[7 Oct-12]

Life of a

SOLDIER

To: ALEX FROM: DAN
THANK YOU SO MUCH
VERY PROUD OF (YOU)

Daniel E. Harper

U. S. Military, Retired

Life of a

SOLDIER

© 2011 by Daniel E. Harper

Harper Press

Temple Hill, Maryland

Published by:

Harper Press

6314 Brinkley Court

Temple Hill, Maryland 20748

While the author has made every effort to provide accurate telephone numbers and internet address at the time of publication, neither the publisher nor the author assumes any responsibility for errors, or for changes that occurs after publication.

Life of a SOLDIER

Copyright © 2011 by Daniel E. Harper

Book design by: Joe Inglima, Atlanta

Printed by: United Book Press, Inc., Baltimore

This book is an original publication of HARPER PRESS

ISBN: 978-1-4276-5198-3

An application to register this book for cataloging has been submitted to the Library of Congress.

PRINTED IN THE UNITED STATES OF AMERICA

10 9 8 7 6 5 4 3 2 1

DEDICATION

I wish to dedicate this book to my wife, Esther Stroy Harper, my three children, Sabrina, Danny, and Davie; my stepson Kasimu, all my grandchildren and great grandchildren, and all of my nieces & nephews, and all youth all over the world in and out of uniform. I am encouraging you to be the *best that you can be* at all times. I would also like to make a special dedication to my nephew Charles Hooper of Atlanta, Georgia for suggesting and encouraging me to write this book.

Thank you and may God Bless You!!!!

ACKNOWLEDGEMENT

There are many people that I would like to thank for many reasons but to mention them all would take up the entire book. But I must acknowledge some special people that were part of my Army family. The first is career Master Sergeant "Ski" who was my first combat platoon sergeant and Lt. James Harris who was my first combat platoon leader. They were instrumental in advancing my career when I began my military service by giving me several rapid promotions during my service in Korea. Next person I wish to acknowledge is 1st Sergeant Burke who took me under his wings and put me on the right road to being a good soldier as well as prepared me to becoming one of the Army's youngest 1st Sergeants during that era. Also, I wish to acknowledge 1st Sergeant Cowles who continued to groom me in Germany for the tough road ahead, as well as Captain Sherbourne, Col. Seigle, and General William DePuy who allowed me to make combat history in Vietnam. Last but certainly not least, General William C. Westmoreland, Army Chief of Staff, for having so much faith in me and allowing me to reach the Army Senior grade.

TABLE OF CONTENTS

APPENDIX

FORWARD

by:

Mrs. Esther Stroy Harper

"Life Of A Soldier" is a compelling story of Daniel's life in Edgefield, S.C., to his desire of wanting to serve and be at the forefront of fighting and protecting his Country. Some of Daniel's brothers served in the military, but Daniel didn't want to just serve but be a leader among leaders.

I met Daniel Harper in March, 1995 on a Friday night. He called me the next day and we decided to meet the next day on Sunday for brunch. We hit if off right away and before we left, Daniel stated that he was going to be so good to me that I'll ask/beg him to marry me. Well I came close to asking however I waited until Daniel asked me. In the words of my male cousin who met Daniel for the first time, he stated, "Daniel is a gentleman's gentleman". My entire family took a liking to Daniel. We have so much in common, and like the same things. I love spending time with my husband (or as he puts it, I love hanging out with him) He treated me with the utmost respect and he has a great since of humor. I can hear the same joke five times and laugh at it just as loud and hardy the fifth time as I did the first time. He has some tall ones to tell.

While we dated, Daniel never talked about what he did in the service and only made general statements about his time in Vietnam. He never wanted to go to the movies to watch "War Movies" and I couldn't watch any movies that had anything to do with any of the wars on TV if he was home. I never pressed the issue or insisted that he talk about his time in the service, but over the years on our many fishing trips, Daniel would tell bits and pieces of his time in Korea on Pork Chop Hill and Vietnam. When he talked about the medals that he was awarded, I would ask to see them and he realized that a lot of his personal items along with his medals were left with his ex-wife. Once he had the medals and certificates in his possession, Daniel began telling me the stories of how he earned each one.

I realized that my husband is a "WARHERO". Daniel loved his time in the service, despite the danger, he wanted to be at the forefront, leading and making decisions for his men. Daniel is the epithany of the commercials for the Military , "Be All That You Can Be". Daniel joined the Army to be the Best in serving his country. He never asked his soldiers to do anything that he was not willing to do first. He

LED BY example and demonstration, and was affectionately known as "Platoon Daddy" while serving in Vietnam as a Platoon Sargeant. Even after he was injured and spent a number of months in the hospital and at home recovering, Daniel wanted to get back to the frontline.

Daniel is all about family. Shortly after entering the service, he promised his mother that he would never take up smoking and/or drinking and kept his promise throughout his adult life. He is extremely close to his sisters & brothers, especially his sisters and talks with them weekly. He talks with one of his nephews daily, talk weekly with most his nephews & nieces. He has an annual fishing trip with his younger nephews. Charles Hooper, a nephew in Atlanta, who calls 2 – 3 times a week in the morning, suggested that Daniel tell his story and some of his other nephews felt that his story should be told also.

To see his story finally in print, is overwhelming. You will enjoy Daniel's journey from his childhood, his description of his loving parents, his love for his sisters and brothers, and his twenty three plus years in the US Army.

PROLOGUE

For a number of years, each day when I wake up, go to the bathroom and eventually make my way to the medicine cabinet to brush my teeth, shave, and comb my hair, I catch myself in the mirror and my hazed eyes staring back at me, and over the course of only a few seconds I replay and hear a familiar refrain in my mind's eye. While looking at me in the mirror, I think to myself in a half serious and sardonic tone: How did I get here, why am I not crippled, maimed, or missing an arm or a leg or both? And I also wonder, how could it be that as a former army infantryman and tanker that has fought in two bloody wars against vicious and tenacious enemies, in places called Pork Chop Hill[1] and War Zone D[2], that I am not dead when so many others have died and that instead I am here in this bathroom, in the Washington metro area, with a loving caring wife in the next room, four wonderful children, nine grandchildren, a nice house, two expensive cars, and a vintage truck? How could it be that when the arc of my life is taken into consideration that I have somehow managed to survive and live a full, productive, and rewarding life? How could it be, I wonder?

---

[1] Site of brutal battle during the Korean War
[2] Region in Vietnam where many intense battles occurred.

1

It takes only an instant – one or two seconds -for all of these images and thoughts to flash through my mind, and afterwards I relax and smile to myself because by now these episodes are as familiar to me as my own face, and of course, I know exactly how I got here and the answers to all the other related questions asked. I am here and survived and succeeded as a professional soldier, first and foremost because of Jesus Christ and his Father who makes all things possible. I am here because of my father and mother who instilled in me values such as hard work, diligence, persistence, discipline, integrity, and most importantly a philosophy of life involving the interplay of the notions of faith and fate. I am here because of my six older brothers and, especially, my four older sisters who gave me friendship and love and thereby a specific kind of self-confidence vital for success in this world. I am here because of all the essential social and political survival skills I learned as an African American male growing up in the rural south of the 30s, 40s, and 50s. I am here because of several white senior army sergeants that took me under their wings and mentored me into becoming the best soldier I can be. I am here through the accident of luck and chance, that is, certain outcomes in my life would have been entirely different had I been just a second early or a second late, or stood in one particular spot instead of just one or two feet over to another spot. And I am here because all of these factors intertwined with my own will and self determination to not just survive but to also succeed and reach the personal and professional goals I had set for myself in this man's army and in life.

This book is about my 23-plus years military career in the United States Army which began in 1952 and ended in 1975. During that period I was an infantryman or a *grunt*[3] and tanker[4] and rose through the enlisted ranks at a very rapid rate from Private to 1st Sergeant, at times being the youngest soldier in a particular rank in the entire army. I served a tour of duty in Korea as a heavy weapons squad leader with the 7th Infantry Division and experienced intense combat and hand-to-hand fighting on the now infamous Pork Chop Hill. I also did four tours of duty in Vietnam, first as an advisor with a Vietnamese ranger battalion and later as a platoon sergeant and acting platoon leader of an armored cavalry unit of the 1st Infantry Division (Big Red 1) where I also saw heavy combat action. After recovering from being severely wounded in Vietnam, I continued my service in the army with several exemplar organizations such as the

---

[3] Term to describe combat infantryman.
[4] Member of armored vehicle or tank.

largest company in the entire army, the U. S. Army Headquarters Company at Fort Myers, Virginia.

Why this book?

Many excellent and worthy books have been written by soldiers and veterans about their combat experiences in our nation's wars and conflicts. Yet despite the number of books few were done from the perspective of the enlisted soldier and fewer still from that of an African American enlisted soldier. There are several speculations about why stories of enlisted and particularly African American enlisted soldiers have not been published. First, there is the perception held by the public and publishers that books about officers that lead large units and commands, and who make grand sweeping decisions that can determine outcomes of wars and conflicts are more interesting to read or are in greater demand than books about enlisted soldiers who are supposedly relegated to *doing the dirty work* or tasks that are seen as less important. Second, officers generally have better and more extended business, political, and social connections than enlisted personnel, particularly outside the army. As a result, these more extensive connections afford them a much better opportunity to have their stories told than those of enlisted personnel. Lastly, there is a perception held by publishers that the majority white population have little or no interest in any books about African Americans, whether they are officers or enlisted. Consequently, due to perceived lower market demand, main line publishing houses are reluctant to market books about African Americans. And sadly, although African Americans have served in our nation's military since Bunker Hill, there are still large segments of our population, white, black, and others, that believes African Americans have not served in the military in significant numbers, or served in combat positions, or made the necessary sacrifices in blood and with their lives for their country.

I wrote this book, in part, to counter these assertions through the telling of my own story about my 23-plus years career in the United States Army from the perspective of an African American enlisted soldier. In telling my story I hope that I honor all soldiers, officers and enlisted, whites, blacks, and other ethnic groups who have served our country in times of war and peace.

I also wrote this book for my former wife, now deceased, and the three beautiful and wonderful children she has blessed me with whom directly or indirectly had to bear the often difficult burden for my choice to make the army a career. It is not just soldiers who suffer the hardships of war. To some extent, it is our families that assume the greatest costs because of separation, constant uncertainty, and fear for the safety of their fathers, husbands, sons, and daughters. I wrote this book to say to my former wife and children all the things I didn't or couldn't tell them about my life as a soldier because I didn't know how or didn't have the courage. I pray that after reading this book they will have a better understanding about who I was and how I lived with the hope that they will find the grace to forgive my failings as a husband and father.

Although I was married for most of my military career out of respect for the privacy of my wife, now deceased, and our three children, only limited information about them and our sometimes challenging life together are mentioned in this book.

An important disclosure is in order relative to this book. I wrote this book while in my later years. Consequently, at my present age memories fade and certain facts are lost, forever. Another important factor contributing to my loss of memory, especially related to names of certain individuals is a strange paradox that exists in the military.

That is, the bond between soldiers in combat is exceedingly strong. The feelings and relationships go beyond brotherhood as in some cases soldiers have given their lives for their fellow soldiers. However, on the flip side, a soldier you once consider closer to you than a family member can be easily forgotten once he or she is reassigned to another unit. It is as if they never existed. Lastly, due to physical limitations and lack of financial resources, I was unable to conduct the exhaustive research necessary to produce all the names of individuals and places, and the exact dates surrounding certain events. I also relied heavily on the online historical archives of the 7th and 1st infantry divisions, as well as online sources for the history of the Korean and Vietnam wars. I indulge your forgiveness for these inadequacies. However, if I had waited to get everything I needed to write the book, it would have never gotten done.

CHAPTER 1

FATHER-MOTHER-SON-MAN

I was the luckiest child in the world to have had the parents and siblings I had. I was born during the heart of the Great Depression in Edgefield County, South Carolina not far from the state line which borders August, Georgia. By most standards, even today's, Edgefield is considered a small county with a population of just over 4000 residents. When I was born, the county was even smaller, with just over 2500 individuals, more than half of whom were African Americans. Yet Edgefield is proud to boost a number of famous or infamous sons including the bashing confederate General James Longstreet who was Lee's most important generals and right hand up to the end of the Civil War and former congressman, senator, governor, and presidential candidate Strom Thurman who is a legend in the state of South Carolina and elevated to the status of a god in Edgefield. Recent revelations of Thurman's sexual relation with an African American maid which produced a child gives credence to the wildly held belief that he also fathered four other children in Edgefield as a result of his liaison with other

African American women. Later in my military career I got to know Thurman personally as we shared a lot in common. I knew Thurman genuinely respected me and my family as we grew to become close and affectionate friends.

Growing up as a child in nearby Aiken, South Carolina, where my family later relocated, was probably similar to all the other small towns in the rural south with all the usual small town sensibilities. The most predominant fact of the social life in Aiken was that the races were segregated in all its aspects. Your race determined where you were born and lived, your occupation, who your friends were, where you went to school, whom you married, where you sought medical help and from whom, and where you died and would be buried. The prevailing social and political structure found in places like Aiken and the rest of the south, and to some extent, the north, was designed to essentially give whites power and advantage over African Americans through the establishment of Jim Crow laws[5] and the institutionalization of violence and threats of violence. Yet, somehow despite these social, political, and economic constraints, my father and mother managed to navigate well and prosper in this closed racist society and came to own a substantial amount

---

[5] Series of punitive laws passed by mostly southern states to suppress the rights of African Americans.

of land, raise and provide very well for twelve children, and serve as community leaders.

My father, Willie H. Harper, was born in Georgia and migrated to South Carolina early in the 20th Century. He was a very handsome man of medium-height, about 5'8, of medium weight, about 170lbs with a brown complexion and soft brown straight hair. In addition to being a farmer on over 200 acres of land that he owned, he was also a minister and simultaneously served as pastor for two local churches. He was a stern and serious person, and very protective of his children. He was also a very strong man who was not that communicative when I was younger but as I grew, he spent a lot of time with me and told me many things about life that he felt I needed to know in order to succeed and to be a good person and a good man. No one outside of our family white or black was allowed to mistreat his family in any way without receiving his wrath and none did. Although he had little formal education, he had a sharp memory and read the bible daily. As a farmer and pastor, he was also an excellent provider for his family and never did I know hunger nor lack any essential necessities during my childhood. At a very early age I could tell that my father was also respected in the community because occasionally people, black and white,

11

came to him seeking his advice and counsel on a wide range of issues.

My mother, Francis T. Harper, was to me the most beautiful woman in the world. She was born and raised in Graniteville, South Carolina. Her father was African American and her mother was a full-blooded Cherokee Indian. Both of my mother's parents were killed in a buggy accident when she was a young mother and before my birth. My mother was of medium height and weight, and had a light brown complexion and long flowing straight black hair that she allowed me to comb for her on a regular basis.

Like my father, she too was very serious minded, had an excellent memory, and a keen eye for details -- traits I was lucky to inherit from both my parents. My mother rather than my father was the parent who was the closest to the children and the one most likely to show affection. Perhaps because I was the youngest and last of her twelve children, she was closer and more affectionate with me than with some of my siblings. To say that we had a very close relationship would be an understatement; indeed, we had a special relationship that extended beyond my childhood until she died at the age of 88.

In total I had eleven siblings: six brothers (James, Arthur, Jerome, Leroy, Bennie, and Carl) and five sisters (Julia Mae, Vermelle, Lucille, Maggie Jo, and Willie Mae). By the time I was born most of my siblings, especially most of my brothers were already grown and had left the house to pursue their goals. Nearly all of my brothers had entered the army and some of my sisters went to either schools to further their education after high school or had married. Of all my siblings I was the closest to my sister Maggie. As I was the youngest or the *baby* of the family, I received special care and attention from primarily my sisters and especially Maggie. In a sense Maggie became a surrogate mother to me by helping my mother look after me while she, my mother, attended to other chores. As I got older Maggie became a cupid of sorts because she was instrumental in helping to arrange dates for me with various young ladies in our town. I feel no sister or brother could have had a closer or more affectionate relationship than ours. The uniqueness of our relationship would last throughout our lives to this very day.

I didn't know or was as close to my brothers as I was to sisters because by the time I was five, most of my brothers had already left the house to begin their careers. However, all of us became closer as I grew into adulthood. I was the closest to Jerome and Bennie because I found it was easier to communicate with them than with my other brothers, and we had a lot more in common. Jerome was a plumber by trade and spent many years in Ghana as an instructor teaching Africans the plumbing trade. Bennie had moved to Jamaica, New York, a suburb of New York City, and had a habit of always playing practical jokes on people. He also loved baseball and we spent many hours talking and watching games on television during the summers when I visited him. His favorite team was the New York Giants.

Our family lived in a large single-level house located on 281 acres of land just outside of Aiken in the rural section of the county in what people often referred to as *the country*. By most standards we lived well and comfortably. My parents own their pasture land and had income from growing vegetables, cotton, produce, hogs, and cattle. The children were always well dressed, had plenty to eat, and attended a private school which was operated by a Baptist missionary organization. My very first school was the elite Bettis Academy, a segregated school for African American children located in Edgefield County. A most unique educational institution, Bettis was a boarding school that educated students from elementary school through the first two years of junior college. I attended Bettis until my family relocated to

Aiken, in the next county. I was an average student who enjoyed school and got along well with all of my teachers. My first teacher, Ms. Franklin, was a tall beautiful caramel colored woman that I had a crush on for years. When I finally became her student, I was her *teacher's pet*. I greatly enjoyed all the attention and special treatment she gave to the envy of all the other kinds in the class.

One of the most unique aspects of Bettis Academy's academic curriculum was a requirement that all its students learn Pig-Latin. Pig Latin is a language game of alterations played in English. To form the Pig Latin form of an English word the first consonant (or consonant cluster) is moved to the end of the word and an *ay* is affixed (for example, *pig* yields *ig-pay* and *computer* yields *omputer-cay*). The purpose of the alteration is to both obfuscate the encoding and to indicate for the intended recipient the encoding as 'Pig Latin'. The reference to Latin is a deliberate misnomer, as it is simply a form of jargon, used only for its English connotations as a 'strange and foreign-sounding language'. It was believed that knowing Pig Latin gave us children and adults a distinct advantage because it allowed us to communicate candidly in public among whites and blacks without fear of repercussions. Children who were not proficient in Pig Latin were considered *bumb bumbs*.

My father, Willie, was indeed the master of the house. He was the primary disciplinarian and presided over all family discussions, and in the end, his was the final word on all matters. Like most families, our dinner time was when we all came together as a family. Meals were special occasions and in our house there was a precise routine we were required to follow during meals. My father always sat at the head of the table and my mother always sat to his immediate left. All dinner plates were turn up-side-down at the beginning and turned over only after prayers were completed. Talking at the dinner table by the children was not allowed unless spoken to by our parents. There was an exact procedure to follow when dinner began. Serving himself first, my father then passed the serving bowls and plates starting from his right with my mother being the last to receive them to his left. During dinners, our parents would observed the manner in which we were eating and make appropriate comments about our appearances, the way we sat, held utensils, chewed our food, and the goodness of the food. One of the most important rituals we always observed was to have had desert at the end of every meal.

After Bettis Academy and when my family relocated a few miles away to Aiken, South Carolina, I attend a number of public segregated schools including Schofield High

School. Schofleid was a relatively large school, with over 500 students, and like most black schools in the south, it was largely underfunded, understaffed, and underequipped relative to the high school the white kids attended. Yet, despite these limitations, on a number of dimensions it was a great institution and I received an excellent education. What Schofield lacked in funding, or equipment, or facilities, relative to the white school, it was more than compensated for by its excellent and dedicated faculty and staff that cared for its student and who always seem to go the extra mile to help us succeed. In time, my parents reenrolled me into Bettis Academy in Edgefield to complete my high school education because of its better academic performance and its reputation for helping children realize higher academic achievement and educational attainment.

A great debate has existed since the landmark Brown vs. the Board of Education decision by the U. S. Supreme Court which effectively ended the segregation of all public schools. The debate is whether the integration of previously segregated schools has been positive for African American children or would it have been more beneficial for African American children to remain in the nurturing and caring environment of segregated schools. Based on my experience at Schofield and Bettis, I personally believe and

17

think the latter would have been a better option for some of our black children today

Aiken was, and is, a mostly segregated community but two of my best friends while growing up were white kids named Furman and Leonard White. Although they went to a different school (the white high school) we were nearly constant companions until we left high school. What was unusual for that period was if they were at my house when it was lunch or supper time, they were invited and ate with my family at the dinner table. The converse was also true, that is, if I was at their house, their parents would invite me to have meals with them. But, we were of different races and there were certain boundaries neither they nor I could or would cross, especially when it came to dating girls.

I understood early in my childhood what the rules and boundaries were in Aiken that governed the relationship between whites and blacks. I've often wonder how did I learn or know this? How did I know what was expected of me in the community? For example, I don't recall my parents or siblings ever telling or explaining to me what I should or shouldn't do relative to whites, yet somehow I instinctively knew.

Perhaps we learn about culture and customs, and the rules that determine how people should interrelate with each other according to race the way we learn language as a child. As a child no one instructs or gives us language lessons on how to speak English. Language is learned instinctively and intuitively through listening, observing, and practicing. Perhaps I learned about racial differences and expected social norms without being taught by anyone, but instead by listening, observing, and through how things I heard and saw made me feel. For example, if it *felt* good, then the thing was good and I would adopt or accept it; and if it *felt* bad then the thing was bad and would learn to reject and not accept.

Ironically, despite the racial and social conditions at the time in Aiken, and throughout the south, my parents taught me and the rest of brothers and sisters another important lesson that has served me well. Growing up, I saw and heard many instances of racial bigotry by whites toward blacks. I knew we were looked upon by whites as, at best, second class citizens, and worst, as animals. But growing up, I never heard my parents say nor did they allow us children to say anything negative or derogatory about whites or the white race. We were taught to be racially tolerant, to treat everyone with dignity, equality and respect, and that in the end were all God's children.

Another key component of my social and emotional training that prepared me for my future as a professional soldier was the philosophical and spiritual training I received as a child growing up in Aiken. Probably more than any other region of the country, the south and its people has a unique understanding and appreciation for the juxtaposition of faith and fate and their relationship with the human condition. For example, if something good or bad happens to someone it is most southern's belief that it was God's intention or will for the good or bad thing to happen to that person. And the end result of what happened was that person's destiny or fate. Consequently, there was no deed to debate or contemplate the issue or matter. It is a *fata compli.*

My acceptance of these belief and principles has served to moderate or mediate the effects of me seeing and experiencing men and women horribly injured or killed in war. Having this spiritual belief and insight about life and death allowed me and other soldiers to have the necessary emotional and psychic strength to endure that horror of what we see in battle and to enable us to live with ourselves afterwards, mostly in peace. Others soldiers I have known that did not have or share this philosophical belief and insight have fared very differently, with some having various forms of emotional and psychological trauma as a result because of their inability to cope with their war experiences. These instincts and lessons would stay with me my entire life and has served me well in the larger world and the army that I soon entered.

I don't recall exactly when I decided to join the army after finishing high school. I hadn't seen any war movies or shows or read any materials that suggested to me that it would be interesting to be a soldier or that the army was a viable career choice. Perhaps it was seeing several of my brothers join the army and come back in uniform that started the idea or it may have been the same reason so many other men and women, blacks and whites, as well as, other races from small southern or rural communities decided to enter. That is, we joined the military not necessarily because we were patriotic or wanted to serve our country in war, or to vanquish our country's enemies. Instead, we joined the military to seek better economic and educational opportunities, to see the world, and to get away from the drudgery of living in small backward towns. The military has always been an important safety valve for young men and women, particular for those of color and from poor backgrounds. Personal histories of service personnel and veterans from small rural towns and modest means are replete with stories of individuals entering the military primarily to seek better opportunities for employment, education and training, personal improvement and well-being, better healthcare, and to further intellectual pursuits. Aiken had little to offer young African American men and women except to work in the fields, mills, or stores as menial laborers and/or as maids, and the town offered nothing to stimulate the cultural and intellectual interests or instincts of young adults. I discussed entering the army with both my parents and all my siblings who were still at home. Everyone knew there was a war going on in Korea and that many men were being killed but all of them gave their quiet approval nonetheless and asked me to be careful.

Through my brothers and others who had served in the army, I had heard many war stories about pitch battles resulting in the deaths of many. Even to me at that age their stories sounded incredulous and difficult to believe. I concluded that the storytellers were probably nowhere near a battlefield and most likely heard the stories from others, or simply fabricated the whole thing. I also concluded that none of the storytellers actual job in the military was in one of the three combat arms and that they were probably just clerks, cooks, drivers, or had one of the many rear echelon jobs that kept them far from the battlefield. In my mind, in order to see *real* action in the military you needed to be in the combat arms, which I resolved to do when I entered the army. I reasoned, combat is where the real soldiers were found and that is where I was determined to be.

CHAPTER 2

TO THE WILD

Upon leaving my high school Bettis Academy, I joined the United States Army in September 1952. The initial enlistment process was begun at an army recruiting station in Aiken, South Carolina. The next day I was taken by bus to Fort Jackson, Columbia, South Carolina for entrance and examination processing. A few days later I was bused to begin Basic Combat Training (BCT) at Camp Breckinridge, Kentucky which was located near the southwestern Indiana city of Evansville.

In retrospect, I was a very green or inexperienced young man at the time I first entered the army. Because most of my brothers had already left the house when I was growing up and my father was inundated with farming and ministerial duties, I lacked sufficient male role models to perhaps adequately prepare me for the army I had entered. I knew if I were to succeed as a soldier, I had a lot of growing up to do and to mature into manhood in a relatively short period of time. I believe this realization and self awareness about my limitations, particularly my inexperience about the workings of the world were critical in preparing me for the challenges to come.

On arrival at Camp Breckinridge I underwent the first right of passage for all recruits in the military: the military hair cut. When I sat in the barber's chair he asked me if I wanted to keep my curly hair or if there was anything special I wanted him to do to my hair. I said I wanted to keep the curls and naively thanked him for asking and for his kind consideration. Without hesitating he gave me the standard *buzz cut* given to all recruits which takes less than 30 seconds or less to complete. As I got up from the chair and walked away, I noticed he was grinning at me like a Cheshire cat. "I hope I did it right for you," he said with a cynical smile.

There is one inexplicable truth about the army. If you work hard, have a good attitude, and do what is expected of you, the world can be your oyster. On the other hand, if you do all or any of the opposite, life in the army can be your worst nightmare. From the start I choose the former. When I entered the army in 1952 I was in the best physical shape of my life. I was eager to learn and took directions easily. I had a positive attitude about life and happy to be where I was - in the army. I also felt a sense of empowerment because for the first time in my life I was far away from home, away from my parents' supervision, and away from all the social constraints of Aiken. I had also received my first pay of $78, which is the most money I had ever earned in my entire life, up to that point. For the first time I truly felt like an independent adult who was out in the world and left to my own devices. I felt wonderful!

After receiving my first pay of $78, I started an allotment which allowed the army to divert a portion of my monthly pay, $40, which would then be mailed to my mother. When I was promoted to Corporal a few months later, the amount of the allotment was increased to $60. Although the money was intended for my mother's use and for her support, she opened a joint bank account in both our names' and deposited the money I was sending for her into that account. Although the money was for her, her intention was to save the money for me. The allotment for my mother stayed in effect from 1952 when I first entered the army until 1975 when she died.

In those days as now all enlisted personnel entering the army had to complete basic combat training or BCT. My BCT unit was K Company, 3rd Battalion, 32nd Regiment,

101st Airborne Division. Completion of BCT was sufficient for a soldier to be assigned to a regular army unit as an infantryman without further training. In those days the army didn't have Advanced Individual Training (AIT) for infantryman as they do today. Thus, unless an individual was destined for one of the other career fields or military occupational specialty (MOS) that required further training or AIT such as medical, mechanic, communication/signal, cook, intelligence, etc., all that was required to become an infantryman was the completion of BCT.

Basic training was 16 weeks and I excelled in all phases of training, including: physical fitness, marksmanship, drill & ceremony, first aid, weapons training, bayonet drills, and various classroom instructions. To my surprise, at the beginning of basic training, I was selected to be the acting platoon sergeant of my platoon of more than 50 men. In addition to having a position of some responsibility, there were also certain perks and privileges that came with the job such as separate living quarters and exemption from pulling the dreaded kitchen police duty or KP in the mess hall. Basic training was tough but it was also very exciting as I was doing and exposed to things I had never before encountered. Again, I loved the training, the fellowship and camaraderie of the men I was with, and admired and respected the leadership of my company and platoon.

In 1952 when I entered the army, the Brown vs. Board of Education decision outlawing segregation in public schools and indirectly everywhere else in American was still two years away and many more years away from full implementation, but the army following, 1947 Executive Order 9981[6] signed by President Harry Truman, had begun, in earnest, to fully integrate its units and the rest of the armed services. One of the drivers for the army to speed up the racial integration of its ranks in the 1950s after dragging its feet since 1948 was the need for more manpower at the start of and during the Korean War. Consequently, the racial integration of my BCT unit at Camp Breckinridge was a direct result of Executive Order 9981 and the army's Korean War manpower shortage.

I was assigned to an integrated BCT unit that consisted of approximately 70% white and 30% African American, most of whom came from the deep south. For most of us, African American and white, sleeping, eating, bathing, working, showering, and competing against one

---

[6] Prior to 1948 it was lawful and expected that races were keep segregated in military units.

another, as equals was a new and bewildering experience for all of us, but the experiment and experience went well and provided the military the impetus and justification to accelerate the process of integrating its ranks.

I concluded that some of the reasons why African Americans and whites worked well together and had a good relation during basic training were that our training was intense and consumed all of our time, leaving less personal time to dwell on our racial differences and the possibility of mischief. Another factor is that all of us knew there was a war going on in Korea and men were being killed, and that in a short period of time some of us or all of us may be sent to Korea to fight as a team. Therefore, it became an imperative that we work together and cooperate as a cohesive unit in order to survive the war and come back in one piece. I believe the other significant factor that helped produce racial harmony and cooperation in the unit was good leadership provided by our officers and NCOs. Historically, the army has always lead the rest of armed services as well as society when striving for racial equality and equal treatment for all its members, irrespective of race, gender, religion, and now sexual orientation. For example, on a percentage basis, the army has always lead the other services in the promotions of African Americans and other minorities to its senior ranks and was the first to promote programs to improve race relations starting in the 70s.

Throughout my army career I had many role models and mentors, comprised primarily of senior noncommissioned officers[7] (NCOs), that provided valuable advice, guidance and insight which were instrumental in the development of my career.

My first mentor was Corporal (CPL) Morrison, an African American soldier who was the assistant platoon sergeant of my BCT unit. Corporal Morrison was also the first soldier I had met that had served in Korea as an infantryman, and I spent hours listening to him talk about his combat experiences. Although I was primarily interested in hearing about the actual fighting and the gore that resulted from combat, he spent most of the time explaining to us how to avoid trouble and to keep from getting killed. He would

---

[7] Noncommissioned officers (NCO) includes all grades of corporal and sergeant; in some countries, warrant officers also carry out the duties of NCOs. The naval equivalent includes some or all grades of petty officer, although not all navies class their petty officers as NCOs. There are different classes of non-commissioned officer, including junior non-commissioned officers (JNCO) and senior (or staff) non-commissioned officers (SNCO).

always say to us, "be sure to always keep your eyes open…" He took time to speak with us because he knew many of us immediately after completing BCT would be headed to Korea to fight. Yet despite his warnings and foreboding stories, my head was filled with the glory of fighting, of being in combat against enemy soldiers, and coming home in triumph. For better or for worst I was eager to go to Korea!

One day in the latter part of our 16 week basic training cycle a formation, gathering all the troops, was called. After we had assembled we were told that the purpose of the formation was to tell each of us where we would be assigned upon completion of the BCT. One by one each person's name was read out loud followed by the assignment. "Jones, Cook School"… "Miller, Supply School"…" Harper, Infantry, Congratulation you got what you wanted, you're going to Korea!"

At graduation from basic training in December 1952, I received orders for Korea and a 15-days leave. I was proud of my performance in basic training where I had excelled in every aspect of training and prouder still of the recognition I received having been appointed acting platoon sergeant. I also reflected upon the training I had with white soldiers in my unit and how well I had performed in comparison. In

Aiken, African Americans were rarely given the opportunity to compete directly against whites in any venue, such as sporting events, because of the fear by whites that if they lost, then the myth of African American inferiority would be brought into questioned, even destroyed. I also contemplated on the positive values of having a racially integrated army as I had seen that people of different colors and ethnicities could work effectively together and change forever the status quo regarding race in our society.

I made my way back to Aiken to begin my 15-days leave. I hadn't seen my parents and some of my siblings for over four months and I was anxious to reunite with them again. My family and friends knew that after my leave I was shipping out to Korea but rarely did anyone bring up the issue that the area was a very active war zone and that I would be in harm's way.

I used most of the 15-days leave visiting with family and friends in South Carolina. During the latter part of the leave I had returned to Aiken to be with my parents and my new girlfriend. On my last day at home I said goodbye to my mother who was having difficulty accepting my departure. I promised her that I would never drink, use alcohol, smoke, use drugs, or gamble and throughout my career in the army I kept that promise. My father then drove me to Augusta, Georgia where I boarded the train bound for San Francisco, California.

Once I arrived in San Francisco I had to clear various administrative procedures before deploying but left in only 2 or 3 days for the army's personnel processing center in Yokohama, Japan. In San Francisco I saw several black men standing near the corner of a building and approached them to say hello. After greeting then, I received no reply or acknowledgement and walked away a little insulted. I discovered later that the soldiers I met were Ethiopians, who were also headed to Korean[8], and some of them didn't speak English, except for the officers who were fluent. After a few more days in Japan, I boarded a troop ship for Pusan, South Korea. I remembered thinking on the ship transiting to Korea that the weather was cool but still very nice in Aiken, even in January. I then wondered to myself if winters were as nice in Korea.

---

[8] In addition to the United States, several other countries supplied military troops for the Korean War including Canada, Ethiopia, Thailand, Australia, and Turkey.

CHAPTER 3

KOREA & THE HEART OF DARKNESS

Korean War began in June 1950 when Soviet backed North Korea crossed the 38th parallel and invaded the American-backed South Korea. The United Nations quickly condemned the invasion as an act of aggression, demanded the withdrawal of North Korean troops from the South, and called upon its members to aid South Korea. In June, President Truman authorized the use of American land, sea, and air forces in Korea; later, the United Nations placed the forces of 15 other member nations under U.S. command, and Truman appointed Gen. Douglas MacArthur supreme commander.

In the first weeks of the conflict the North Korean forces met little resistance and advanced rapidly. By September they had driven the South Korean army and a small American force to the Busan (Pusan) area at the southeast tip of Korea. A counteroffensive began on Sept.

15, when UN forces made a daring landing at Incheon on the west coast. North Korean forces fell back and MacArthur received orders to pursue them into North Korea. On October, the North Korean capital of Pyongyang was captured; by November, North Korean forces were driven by the 8th Army, under Gen. Walton Walker, and the X Corp, under Gen. Edward Almond, almost to the Yalu River, which marked the border of Communist China. As MacArthur prepared for a final offensive, the Chinese Communists joined with the North Koreans to launch a successful counterattack. The UN troops were forced back, and in January 1951, the Communists again advanced into the South, recapturing Seoul, the South Korean capital.

After months of heavy fighting, the center of the conflict was returned to the 38th parallel, where it remained for the rest of the war. MacArthur, however, wished to mount another invasion of North Korea. When MacArthur persisted in publicly criticizing U.S. policy, Truman, on the recommendation of the Joint Chiefs of Staff removed him from command and installed Gen. Matthew B. Ridgway as commander in chief. Gen. James Van Fleet then took command of the 8th Army. Ridgway began truce negotiations with the North Koreans and Chinese, while small unit actions, bitter but indecisive, continued. Gen. Van

Fleet was denied permission to go on the offensive and end the "meat grinder" war.

I arrived in port city of Pusan, South Korea on January 10th, 1953. It was the dead of winter and the air was the coldest I had ever experienced and heavy with moisture. I was in Pusan for only the few days it took to process me in-country and to be assigned to my permanent unit. The massive American and United Nation's military presence was evident everywhere I turned. Personnel, vehicles, and a wide assortment of materials and crates where stacked in massive piles reaching to the sky. I was cloistered while at Pusan so I didn't see the towns, villages, and people until I was transported, by truck heading north, first to the headquarters' of the 8th Corps and later to the 7th Infantry Division for assignment to my permanent unit.

The 7th Infantry Division was originally activated in 1917 and served in World War One. Although elements of the division saw brief active service in World War One, it is best known for its participation in the pacific during World War Two where it took heavy casualties engaging the Imperial Japanese Army in the Aleutian Islands, Leyte, and Okinawa.

Following the Japanese surrender in 1945, the division was stationed in Japan and Korea, and with the outbreak of the Korean War in 1950 was one of the first units in action. It took part in the Inchon Landings and the advance north until Chinese forces counter-attacked and almost overwhelmed the scattered division. The 7th later went on to fight in the Battle of Pork Chop Hill and the Battle of Old Baldy.

At the outbreak of the Korean War in 1950, the 7th Infantry Division commander, Major General David G. Barr, assembled the division at Camp Fuji near Mount Fuji. The division was already depleted due to post-war shortages of men and equipment and further depleted as it sent large numbers of reinforcements to strengthen the 25th Infantry Division and 1st Cavalry Division, which were sent into combat in South Korea in July. The division was reduced to 9,000 men, half of its wartime strength. To replenish the ranks of the under strength division, the Republic of Korea assigned over 8,600 poorly trained Korean soldiers (KATUSA) to the division. With the addition of priority reinforcements from the US, the division was eventually increased to 25,000 when it entered combat. Also fighting with the 7th Infantry Division for much of the war were members of the three successive Kagnew Battalions sent by the nation of Ethiopia as part of the United Nations forces.

On November 25, 1951 Chinese forces entered the war against the United Nations, advancing across the Manchurian border and attacking the Eighth Army's IX Corps and South Korean II Corps in the west and X Corps in the east. X Corps found itself under attack from the 20th, 26th and 27th Chinese field armies, commanding a total of 12 divisions. During the furious action that followed, the 7th Infantry Division's spread out regiments were unable to resist the overwhelming Chinese forces. Three of the Division's infantry battalions were attacked from all sides the next day. 1st Battalion, 32nd Infantry (nicknamed Task Force Faith) was trapped with two other battalions by the 80th and 81st Chinese infantry divisions from the 27th Field Army. In the subsequent Battle of Chosin Reservoir, the three battalions were destroyed by overwhelming Chinese forces suffering over 2,000 casualties. The 31st Infantry suffered heavy casualties trying to fight back the Chinese forces further north, but the 17th Infantry was spared of heavy attack, retreating along the Korean coastline, out of range of the offensive. By the time X Corps ordered a retreat, most of the 7th Infantry Division, save the 17th Infantry Regiment, had suffered 40 percent casualties. The scattered elements of the division saw repeated attacks as they attempted to withdrawal to the port of Hungnam in December 1950. These attacks cost the division another 100 killed before it was fully evacuated. The division suffered 2,657 killed and 354 wounded during the retreat. Most of the dead were members of Task Force Faith.

The division returned to the front lines in early 1951, spearheaded by the 17th Infantry, which had suffered the fewest casualties from the Chinese offensive. Division elements advanced through Tangyang in South Korea, and blocking enemy offensives from the northwest. The division reached full strength and saw action around Cheehon, Chungju, and Pyongchang as part of an effort to push the North Korean and Chinese forces back above the 38th parallel and away from Seoul. The 7th Infantry Division engaged in a series of successful limited objective attacks in the early weeks of February, a series of small unit attacks and ambushes between the two sides. By the end of the month the 17th Infantry was driving against a ridge near the village of Maltari. It would continue slowly advancing and clearing enemy hilltop positions through April. By April the entire Eighth Army was advancing north as one line stretching across the peninsula, reaching the 38th parallel by May. The division, assigned to IX Corps, then assaulted and fought a fierce three-day battle culminating with the recapture of the terrain that had been lost near the Hwachon Reservoir just over the 38th parallel in North Korea. In capturing the town bordering on the reservoir it cut off thousands of enemy troops. The division fought on the front lines until June 1951 when it was assigned to the reserve for a brief rest and refitting.

When the division returned to the lines in October, after another assignment in reserve, it moved to the Heartbreak Ridge sector recently vacated by the 2nd Infantry Division, where it was supported by the 3rd Infantry Division and 1st Cavalry Division. During this new deployment the division fought in the Battle for Heartbreak Ridge, to take an area of staging grounds for the Korean and Chinese armies. It remained static in the region until February 23, 1952 when it was sent into reserve and relieved by the 25th Infantry Division. The next year saw the 7th Division engaged in an extended campaign for nearby land, the Battle of Old Baldy. The 7th Division continued to defend "Line Missouri" through September 1952, though it became known as the "Static Line" as UN forces made few meaningful gains in the time.

The 7th Infantry Division's Operation Showdown launched in the early morning hours of October 14, 1952, with the 31st Infantry and 32nd Infantry at the head of the attack. The target of the assault was the Triangle Hill complex northeast of Kumhwa. The 7th Infantry Division remained in the Triangle Hill area until the end of October, when it was relieved by the 25th Infantry Division. The 7th Infantry Division was highly praised by commanders for its tenacity through the fight.

The division continued patrol activity around Old Baldy Hill and Pork Chop Hill into 1953, digging tunnels and building a network of outposts and bunkers on and around the hill. In April, the North Korean Army began stepping up offensive operations against UN forces. During the Battle of Pork Chop Hill, the Chinese 67th and 141st divisions overran Pork Chop Hill using massed infantry and artillery fire. The hill had been under the control of the 31st Infantry. The 31st counterattacked with reinforcements from the 17th Infantry and recaptured the area the next day. On July 6 the North Koreans and Chinese launched a determined attack against Pork Chop resulting in five days of fierce fighting with few meaningful results. By the end of July, five infantry battalions from the 31st and 17th were defending the hill, while a

Chinese division was in position to attack it. During this standoff, the UN ordered the 7th Infantry Division to retreat from the hill in preparation for an armistice, which would end major hostilities.

During the Korean War, the division saw a total of 850 days of combat, suffering 15,126 casualties, including 3,905 killed in action and 10,858 wounded. For the next few years, the division remained on defensive duty along the 38th parallel, under the command of the Eighth Army

I was assigned to K Company, 3rd Battalion, 32nd Regiment, 7th Infantry Division. Within a few months I received several rapid promotions to Private First Class (PFC) in February, Corporal (Cpl) in March, and to Sergeant on May 26th. As sergeant, probably the youngest in the entire army. I was leader of a heavy weapons squad of eleven men. There were four whites, two African Americans, one Hispanics, and four KATUSA who were native Koreans assigned to American army units. Three squad members I remember distinctly include Campos, a Mexican-American from Corpus Christi, Texas who taught me a little Spanish; Blue, an African-American from North Carolina, and interestingly another soldier named (Ronald) Harper who frequently entertained us with his guitar.

An incident occurred early in my deployment which signaled an improvement or a shift in the prevailing paradigm of race relations among soldiers. My squad which was comprised of men of different races was in a truck moving to a new position. One of the soldiers pulled out a gallon can of tomato juice and to share it with others. Without hesitation men who were black, white, brown, and yellow all proceeded to drink from the same can as it was being passed around. It was the first time I had seen people, especially blacks and whites have such close physical contact by essentially exchanging bodily fluids. When I saw this I said to myself that would never happen in Aiken, South Carolina or anywhere else in the south.

The platoon leader, an officer, was First Lieutenant (1LT) James Harris from Georgia who treated all of the men in his platoon with dignity and respect. Years later in the early 1970s when I became 1st Sergeant, I met Harris one day at the Pentagon. He had remained in the army after Korea and by then had reached the rank of full colonel.

Our platoon sergeant was Sergeant "Ski" who took me under his wings. We called him "Ski" because he had a long Polish name which was difficult to pronounce. When I first joined the platoon he once told me, "young soldier, I like

44

what I see in you... you'll make a good soldier." Doug Wilder, who would later become the first African American governor of Virginia, had also been in the same company as an officer and fought at Pork Chop Hill, although a short time earlier. In later years we became close friends and I attended and participated in all of Governor Wilder's inaugural activities when he was sworn in 1990.

My first impressions from what I initially saw in Korea matched none of my preconceived notions of what a war zone should look like. The harsh winter and extreme cold made the land appear worst, like something entirely surreal and not of this world. But it was this world. There were places that looked like a nightmarish lunar landscape with bare lifeless open ground spaces scattered with bomb craters, and punctuated with scared and battered trees and dead colorless brush.

Both the villages and the people I saw and encountered looked like they were living in a medieval period, which was true, and I wondered how they could survive in this place. Even in the middle of the day, it looked and felt like it was midnight. It was like something out of a Joseph Conrad's novel. Most of the people live in nothing more than shanty towns with homes and other structures made from whatever materials that could be scavenged from garbage dumps. The clothes I saw most people wore were made from U. S. Army blankets with the initials "US" still visible on the material. It seemed none of the bare essentials were available to the people such as food, medicine, and shelter unless obtained through a thriving black market. Also thriving were the illicit trades, such as prostitution, gambling, smuggling, and drug trafficking, which seem to be the only viable economic system in the country. It is said you can tell the morals of a society by what the people ate. In that regard, I am to this day still troubled by seeing the Korean people literally eating garbage and other scrapes they could find such as dogs and other four legged animals. It was sad and heartbreaking to witness the impact of war on ordinary people, especially those who are the weakest: the old, the women and the children; their only survival strategy was to beg from sun up to sun down. It was, indeed, hell on earth.

There was something else about the Korean people. Their seemingly backwardness demeanor and the constant look of fear on their faces reflected, I believe, the many years and generations they spent being a conquered people, first by the Mongols, then the Chinese, and finally the Japanese. There was no look of defiance or anger on their faces, just fear, defeatism, and a resolve that it was better to simply survive and live under any system, even as a slave, than to fight.

Today, Korea is an economic superpower because of the determination and industry of its people. I am sure their motivation to succeed was, in part, driven by the deprivation they experienced and remembered as a nation and as a people during the Korean War.

I also met many foreign troops fighting under the auspices of the United Nations, including Ethiopians, whose officers were required to speak three languages, Turks, Thais, Canadians, as well as others. The Turks carried long knives on their sides that were sharp enough to use as a razor to shave facial hair. They were quiet and fierce fighting men but very friendly and open. Their main diet was a fish called a mudden (sp), which they ate as often as they could. The Canadians were a closely knit group but were also very friendly and they invited me to visit them if and when the war was over.

My battalion was based at Camp Bayonet just northeast of Seoul and north of the 38th parallel. Despite ongoing truce negotiations the level of fighting between the allies and the North Korean and Communist forces was still very intense and resulted in large causalities on both sides. During the period between my assignment to my permanent unit in January and early July of 1953, my squad and rest of the company were primarily either on patrol or in fixed defensive positions in foxholes or bunkers along the main line of resistance (MLR) or the front lines facing the enemy. It was the middle of winter and the physical misery caused by the coldness, compounded by the rain, snow, and the winds was more than anything I had ever experienced in my life. Many soldiers suffered cold related injuries such as hyperthermia and frost bite and it seemed no matter how many layers of clothing one wore or how close one got to a make shift fire burning in an empty 52 gallon drum, the cold never abated, it never left. Day after day, fully exposed to the elements, the cold sunk deep down into my bones and stayed. I remember many a times shivering with cold and hoping and praying that an enemy soldier or anyone would come by and shoot me to put me out of my misery. It was miserable and I remember distinctly then thinking whether it was still a good idea that I joined the army after all.

My first experience witnessing death in battle occurred during this period and while on my first patrol. My patrol had come under fire from the Chinese and we hit the dirt as fast as we could. My sergeant who led the patrol yelled out to us that no one should move from where they were no matter what the circumstances to prevent giving the enemy an easy shot. A soldier in the patrol asked "what if I have to go to the bathroom?" Sergeant Ski reiterated what he said, "No one moves!"

The weather was bitterly cold and wet, and after some length of time when it seemed that the danger had passed, a lieutenant in the company, a very large man from Texas, stood up to shake the cold and cramps out of his legs. The intent seemed innocent enough, but as soon as he stood up a gunshot was heard followed by a moan as he fell dead next to me. The event shocked me for a moment as I looked at his body and then face. A life gone just like that, in an instant. There would be no second chance for him and I remember thinking how glad I was that it wasn't me lying dead on that frozen ground in the middle of nowhere, halfway around the world from my home, family, and friends. My remorse for the lieutenant lasted for only a few seconds because I reasoned it his fate to die at this time, at this place, and in this manner. That somehow it was all part of God's master plan and therefore, just.

Despite the shock of seeing before my eyes a life taken away so easily and suddenly, the immediate aftermath was even more personally disturbing and horrific. I was assigned to carry the dead officer's body down a hill on a litter along with another soldier. Because it had rained the night before and all that day, the ground was muddy and slippery, making it difficult to get a firm footing. For what seemed like eternity, we carried the body down the hill, slipping, sliding, and falling as we went. As we fell many times, the body rolled off the stretcher landing on the muddy ground in as many times. With great difficult and anguish we replaced the body back on the stretcher only to repeat the process of slipping, falling, replacing, and moving a few more steps down the hill. The cold made the dead lieutenant's body feel heavier and heavier too were our feelings of desperation, fear, sorrow, and despair.

It was also during this time that, for the first time, I had killed an enemy soldier. Four men from my squad and I were on patrol near the MLR walking down a path through a slightly wooded area. The point man for the patrol noticed movement ahead and we quickly took cover on the ground and behind trees. A Chinese soldier, his unit's point man, suddenly came into view slowing walking along the same dirt path bent over in a crouch. I remember my heart pounding so hard in my chest I thought the whole world could hear it. As the Chinese came closer and was about 50 yards away I took aim with my M1 Garand rifle and squeeze off one round and then two and then the entire eight round clip. The Chinese solder stood upright for a moment and then, seemingly in slow motion, as if to avoid the inevitable, fell forward, with a look of utter surprise and confusion, landing on his face. Dead. When the shooting had stopped we could see that the other members of his patrol had fled. We waited a few more minutes and then we approached the dead body. The blood had poured onto the ground surrounding him. We poked his body with a rifle to ensure that he was dead and grabbed his weapon and returned to our base.

When I first arrived in Korea, I was afraid of what was ahead of me. I knew I could be killed and never again see my family and friends. I don't know how I overcame my fear at first. Often before heading out on patrols knowing we may run into the enemy, my legs felt like rubber bands, my stomach ached, my vision narrowed, my head would spin. I also saw how fear impacted others. I saw soldiers urinated and defecated in his pants, and the ones who could move, often remaining in a fetal position crying like a baby, or the ones who froze at their positions unable to fire their weapons even thought the enemy was advancing and destined to kill them. At first I simply *willed* myself into performing my duties as a soldier. For me, the fear of being seen a coward was the chief motivating factor.

The focus of my fear about combat changed when I was put into a leadership position as a squad leader. Strangely my new fear was not for my own personal safety and well being but rather the fear which stems from failing as a leader in the eyes of my men, failing to carry out my duties, and failing to keep my men safe. The transposition of my fear from one source to another was liberating and made me a much more effective soldier and leader as I was able to make decision as a squad leader and not be influenced by any potential personal danger.

The war in Korea was bloody and vicious. The North Korean and Chinese soldiers were responsible for the deaths of thousands of American and UN forces as well as Korean citizens who were noncombatants. Because of seeing men I knew died in battle I felt no particular remorse or pity for the soldiers I had killed. I didn't think about their families and their loss and I didn't think about them suffering as they died or the life they would have lived. If I could have I would have killed as many enemy soldiers as possible, emptying a full rifle clip into each one. I thought I am a soldier and this is what a soldier does in war.

By January 1953 the war in Korea had raged on for just over two-and-half years and was at a stalemate. The principal battles of the stalemate include the Battle of Bloody Ridge; the Battle of Heartbreak Ridge; the Battle of Old Baldy; the Battle of White Horse; the Battle of Triangle Hill; the Battle of Hill Eerie; the sieges of Outpost Harry; and for me, the Battle of Pork Chop Hill.

The Battle of Hill 255 of which Pork Chop Hill was one of several out cropping of this complex of hills comprises a pair of related Korean War infantry battles during the spring and summer of 1953. It was called Pork Chop Hill because the contours on the map used by US/UN forces resembled a pork chop. The battles in and around Hill 255, which included Pork Chop Hill, were fought while the U.S. and the Communist Chinese and Koreans negotiated an armistice. In the U.S., they were controversial because of the many soldiers killed for terrain of no strategic or tactical value. The first battle was described in the eponymous history French Fries' Hill: The American Fighting Man in Action, Korea, Spring 1953, by S.L.A. Marshall, from which the film Pork Chop Hill was drawn.

The hill, 300 meters high, was first seized by the U.S. 8th Cavalry in October 1951, again in May 1952 by Item Company of the U.S. 180th Infantry, then defended by the 21st Thai Battalion of the 2nd Infantry Division (United States) in November, 1952. Since December 29, 1952, the outpost was part of the 7th Infantry Division's defensive sector. Pork Chop Hill, itself, was one of several exposed hill outposts in front of the Main Line of Resistance (MLR), defended by a single company or platoon positioned in sand-bagged bunkers connected with trenches.

Opposing the 7th Infantry Division were two divisions of the Chinese Communist Forces: the 141st Division of the 47th Army, and the 67th Division of the 23rd Army. These were veteran, well-trained units expert in night infantry assaults, patrolling, ambushes, and mountain warfare. Both armies (Corps-equivalent units) were part of the 13th Field Army commanded by General Deng Hua, who was also deputy commander of Chinese Volunteer Army forces in Korea.

The opposing forces in this sector were roughly equal in size, the 7th Division (Major General Arthur Trudeau, commanding) totaling 11 infantry battalions (including attached battalions from Colombia and Ethiopia), a battalion of armor, and 6 battalions of artillery, while the Chinese forces totaled 12 infantry, 10 artillery, and the equivalent of one tank battalion.

Both the United Nations Command and the Chinese had used military operations to gain leverage or make political statements relevant to the armistice negotiations since early 1952. The first battle on Pork Chop Hill occurred near Operation Little Switch, the exchange of ill and injured prisoners-of-war scheduled for April 20. The Chinese command authorized the April attack to demonstrate that agreement in contentious negotiations did not equal unwillingness to continue fighting, if necessary.

In a surprise night attack on March 23, 1953, a battalion of the Chinese 423rd Regiment, 141st Division seized an outpost near Pork Chop Hill called "Old Baldy" (Hill 266) and quickly overwhelmed B Company of the 31st Infantry's Colombian Battalion, commanded by Lt. Colonel Alberto Ruiz Novoa, during its relief in the Fifth Battle for Old Baldy. 31st Infantry Regiment Commander Colonel William B. Kern had ordered C Company of the Colombian Battalion to relieve B Company despite the Colombian commander's protest. The attack caught both companies amidst the rotation. Two days of heroic resistance by the maimed and battered B and C companies failed in retaking the hill due to the failure of the 31st Regiment commander to send reinforcements, causing the United Nations Command to order its abandonment. This preliminary fight exposed Pork Chop to three-sided attack, and, for the next three weeks, Chinese patrols probed it nightly.

On the night of April 16, Company E, 31st Infantry manned Pork Chop Hill. Shortly before midnight, an artillery barrage foreshadowed a sudden infantry assault by a battalion of the Chinese 201st Regiment; Pork Chop Hill was quickly overrun, although pockets of U.S. soldiers defended isolated bunkers. Elsewhere in the sector, other positions were attacked, pressuring the entire 7th Division.

Company K and Company L, 31st Infantry, in reserve behind the MLR, were ordered to counterattack and began their attack at 04:30 on April 17. By dawn they reached the main trenches on top of the hill but suffered almost 50% casualties, and half of Company L's troops had not been able to leave the trenches of an adjacent outpost, Hill 200. Lt. Clemons, in tactical command of the assault, requested reinforcement. 2nd Battalion 17th Infantry was already attached to the 31st Infantry and its Company G (1st Lt. Walter B. Russell) was immediately sent forward, linking up with Company K at 08:30. All three companies were subjected to almost continuous shelling by CCF artillery as they cleared bunkers and dug in again.

Through a series of miscommunications between command echelons, Division headquarters ordered Russell's company to withdraw at 15:00 after they too had suffered heavy losses, and did not realize the extent of casualties among the other two companies. By the time the situation was clarified the companies of the 31st Infantry were down to a combined 25 survivors. Maj. Gen. Trudeau, by then on scene, authorized Col. Kern to send in a fresh company to relieve all elements on Hill 255 and placed him in tactical command with both the 1st and 2nd Battalions of the 17th Infantry attached and at his direction.

Kern sent forward Company F, 17th Infantry, which started up the hill at 21:30 under heavy artillery fire but reached the trenches at 22:00, suffering 19 killed in the process. Kern at 23:00 then ordered Company E, 17th Infantry, to move up to reinforce Company F. Smith, to avoid the bulk of the artillery fire, moved around the right flank of the hill and up the side facing the Chinese positions

Company K, 31st Infantry had incurred 125 casualties, including 18 killed, of its original 135 men. After twenty hours of steady combat the remaining seven members started off the hill singly just after midnight of April 17–18 and withdrew without further losses. Several of Company L's survivors remained with the relief troops to familiarize them with the layout of the hill defenses.

During the early morning of April 18, the Chinese 201st Regiment renewed its attack at 01:30 and again inflicted heavy losses on the defenders, nearly overrunning Company F in battalion strength. The timely counterattack by Company E, 17th Infantry caught the Chinese by surprise on their flank and ended the organized assault. The 141st Division renewed attacks in company strength at 03:20 and 04:20 but did not gain further ground.

At dawn on April 18, an additional U.S. rifle company (Company A, 17th Infantry) climbed the hill to reinforce the 2nd Battalion companies. Together the three companies spent the bulk of the day clearing the trenches and bunkers of all hiding Chinese and securing the hilltop. The battle ended that afternoon.

UN artillery had fired over 77,000 rounds in support of the three outposts attacked, including nearly 40,000 on Pork Chop Hill alone on April 18; the Chinese expended a similar amount.

Both the Chinese and U.S. infantry assaulted the hill initially under cover of a moonless night. Each used a heavy preparatory artillery barrage to force the defenders to cover in bunkers and to screen the approach of the attacking troops. Chinese forces used rapid movement and infiltration tactics to close quickly on the trenches and surprise the defenders, while the US forces used grazing fire (small arms fire placed approximately 1–2 feet above the ground surface) to limit defensive small arms fire, then maneuvered systematically up the hillsides under shellfire. Neither side employed supporting fire from tanks or armored personnel carriers (APC) to protect attacking troops.

Once inside the trench line, troops of both forces were forced to eliminate bunkers individually, using hand grenades, explosive charges, and occasionally flame throwers, resulting in heavy casualties to the attackers. For the UN forces, infiltration of cleared bunkers by bypassed Chinese was a problem throughout the battle and hand-to-hand combat was a frequent occurrence.

Evacuation of casualties was made hazardous by almost continuous artillery fires from both sides. The 7th Division made extensive use of tracked M-39 APC's to evacuate casualties and to protect troops involved in the resupply of water, rations, and ammunition, losing only one during the battle. In addition the UN forces employed on-call, pre-registered defensive fires called flash fire to defend its outposts, in which artillery laid down an almost continuous box barrage in a horseshoe-shaped pattern around the outpost to cover all approaches from the Chinese side of the MLR.

U.S. losses were 104 dead, including 63 in the 31st Infantry, 31 in the 17th Infantry and 10 among engineers and artillery observers, and 373 wounded. Chinese losses were unknown.

The 7th Division rebuilt its defenses on Pork Chop Hill in May and June, 1953, during a lull in major combat. Final agreements for an armistice were being hammered out and the UN continued its defensive posture all along the MLR, anticipating a cease-fire in place.

On the night of July 6, using tactics identical to those in the April assault, the Chinese again attacked Pork Chop.

The hill was now held by Company A, 17th Infantry, under the temporary command of 1st Lt. Richard T. Shea, Jr, its executive officer. Company B of the same regiment, in ready reserve behind the adjacent Hill 200, was immediately ordered to assist, but within an hour, Company A reported hand-to-hand combat in the trenches. A major battle was brewing and division headquarters ordered a third company to move up. The battle was fought in a persistent monsoon rain for the first three days, making both resupply and evacuation of casualties difficult. The battle is notable for its extensive use of armored personnel carriers in both these missions.

On the second night, the Chinese made a new push to take the hill, forcing the 7th Division to again reinforce. Parts of four companies defended Pork Chop under a storm of artillery fire from both sides. At dawn of July 8, the rain temporarily ended and the initial defenders were withdrawn. A fresh battalion, the 2nd Battalion of the 17th, counter-attacked and re-took the hill, setting up a night defensive perimeter.

In early July 1953 my unit was assembled and told we are moving out to Pork Chop Hill. On July 8th, we were trucked to the base of Pork Chop Hill and then loaded unto M-39 armored personnel carriers (APCs) used during World War II. Although we were some distance from the fighting we could hear many small rounds, mortars, and heavy artillery fire. The APCs loaded with 4-6 men proceed to drive up to and then along the ridge of the hill toward a system of earthen bunkers and entrenchments that were already built by the US and UN forces that meandered throughout Pork Chop Hill complex.   The short trip from the foot of the hill to the unloading point at the entrance of one of the entrenchment and bunker complex took only 10-15 minutes. Once we got to our destination we immediately came under fire from enemy soldiers. We quickly jumped off the trucks and scrambled to the bunkers to take up our positions. Included in my squad that day was our company's clerk, an Italian American from New York. The clerk gave us permission to call him "WOP," a derogatory term used to describe Italian Americans. He wasn't asked or required to go with us that but he volunteered and insisted he wanted to go with the squad so that he could see "some action." He decision proved fateful.

Our position consisted of a single trench that was approximately 30-40 feet long and six feet wide. On either side of the trench there were rows of bunkers that could hold up to six men. Entrance to the bunkers from the trench side was through a small hole big enough for only one man to use at a time. Facing away from the trench and toward the surrounding hills and ridges, and towards the enemy, each bunker had a single window size hole for gun emplacements.

Enemy soldiers were everywhere. They could be seen from our bunkers 300-500 years away advancing towards. They were also on top of the ridges and crests of hills surrounding our positions as well as directly on top of our positions firing down on us.

My unit and I were at Pork Chop Hill for three days and had constant contact with enemy soldiers who were literally in our mist. During that period we had no sleep, the air in the bunker was horrific, and I was forced to suppress and conceal my own fear and concern for our tactical situation, the vulnerability of our bunkers, and for our safety so as to not demoralize my men. Chinese and North Korean soldiers were below and above our bunkers and could be seen from a distance as they advanced toward our positions. We killed many enemy soldiers with rifle fire and our 30 caliber machinegun. Our company was also taking heavy causalities from Chinese soldiers who also held certain sections of Pork Chop and adjacent hills after they had overrun positions previously held by American and UN forces. The majority of the heavy fighting was done during daylight but intense fighting also occurred throughout night along with large quantities of gunfire, mortar and artillery fire.

The second day at Pork Chop Hill, for us, was like the first except some enemy Chinese soldiers had breached and penetrated the defensive line immediate to the bunkers. The seriousness of the breach was impressed upon me when in the mist of all the shouting, firing, cursing, and bombs exploding all around us a large enemy Chinese soldier, who was probably an ethnic Mongolian and the biggest Asian I had ever seen at over 6 feet and more than 200 pounds, crashed through the weaken wall of our bunker and was preparing to stab or bayonet me with his rifle when suddenly, in a split second, an American soldier from an adjacent bunker fired and killed the Chinese army soldier who fell to my feet. The soldier who saved my life is, of course, someone I will never forget: Master Sergeant George Kuh (sp.) from Hawaii.

By the third day word came down that we were to retreat from Pork Chop Hill because commanders had decided that the military situation there was untenable and once we were off the hill it would be bombed off the face of the earth. For those on the hill and in the trenches retreating from the hill would be just as dangerous as remaining because enemy soldiers had infiltrated most of the positions and could easily fire on retreating soldiers with small arms and mortar fire. But, by then no one wanted to stay and was anxious to begin to regress down the hill.

There were six of us in the bunker that was beginning to collapse in on itself. The only exit was a small hole leading to the trench. As squad leader, and in light of the danger involved in escaping from the bunker and trench we were in, it would have been expected that I would be the first to exit through the hole of the bunker. But I was concerned that if I had escape while all or some my men had been killed leaving the bunker, it would have appeared that I had abandoned them. To avoid the possibility of that happening I agreed to go last.

When I gave the order to "move out" the first man who attempted to go through the hole was our company clerk.

Half way through the hole I heard rapid gunfire and saw that he had been hit. The gunfire was so devastating and destructive that his body was literally torn apart with his torso torn opened exposing his internal organs which then fell unto the ground, and partially blocking the hole from which we were to escape. In a state of disbelief at what had just happened, I hesitated in deciding the next move. When I regained my equanimity I told my men "let's go... get moving." In rapid succession each man subsequently made their way through the hole using their hands and shoulders to crawl through the blood, feces, internal organs, and exposed bones of the dead soldier to enter the trench pathway. After each man had exited, I also made my way through the blood and exposed guts and body part. We did not attempt to retrieve the body parts of the clerk, which would have been impossible to do without shovels and bags.

Covered in blood, feces, multi-day old sweat, we scrambled down the hill under heavy fire. While scurrying down I saw a familiar face on a stretcher. The man on the stretcher was my first cousin Charles Quiller, who days earlier told me, "Boy, don't get yourself killed here while the folks at home are having trouble voting." The stretcher bearer then placed a blanket over his head and carried him away. I was sicken and devastated by the knowledge that my cousin had just died and despite being close to his family I did not have the courage or the strength to write and tell his family about his death. Then off in the distance I could hear the thunder and feel the concussion from exploding bombs being dropped by the air force on the Pork Chop Hill. Despite the number of men that had died on Pork Chop Hill, I wondered how was it that I survived. Whatever the answer, I was glad to be alive.

My impression of the Chinese soldier was that they had very little regard for life, especially their own. They suffered heavy casualties when they conducted full frontal assaults against our entrenched positions, killing hundreds perhaps thousands at a time. Those who survived and were taken prisoner appeared to be from another planet. They were underfed, under-equipped, uneducated, and were startled to be treated like humans and men. Many Chinese prisoners refused repatriation to North Korea and China after the war, many settling in Taiwan instead.

What did Pork Chop Hill costs in terms of lives? Four of the thirteen U.S. company commanders were killed. Total U.S. casualties were 243 killed, 916 wounded, and nine captured. 163 of the dead were never recovered. Of the 206 men in my company before deployment to Pork Chop Hill, only 26 were left and in my squad of ten, four had been killed. Of the Republic of Korea troops ("KATUSA") attached to the 7th, approximately 15 were killed and 120 wounded.

Chinese casualties were estimated at 1,500 dead and 4,000 wounded. Lieutenant Richard Thomas Shea and Cpl. Daniel D. Schoonover, a combat engineer, were both posthumously awarded the Medal of Honor. Within a few days the battalion was back at its base camp where we resumed the routine of manning fixed position toward the MLR and conducting night patrols. And, less than three weeks after the Battle of Pork Chop Hill, the armistice was signed by the United Nations Command (Korea), Chinese Peoples Liberation Army, and North Korean Peoples Army, ending the hostilities.

The Korean War ended July 27, 1953 and I would remain in the country until February 1954 when I was shipped back to the United States. Since my Korean service, I often think about the human and related cost of the war that devastated so many.

According to the data from the U. S. Defense Department, the United States had suffered 33,686 battle deaths, along with 2,830 non-battle deaths during the Korean War and 8,176 missing in action.- Western sources estimate the PVA[9] had suffered between 100,000 to 1,500,000 deaths (most estimate some 400,000 killed), while the KPA[10] had suffered between 214,000 to 520,000 deaths. Between some 245,000 to 415,000 South Korean civilian deaths were also suggested, and the entire civilian casualty during the war were estimated from 1,500,000 to 3,000,000 (most sources estimate some 2,000,000 killed)

Another often untold related human cost of the Korean War was the large number of mixed race 'G.I. babies' (offspring of U.S. and other western soldiers and Korean women) that were produced during the conflict and those which were not killed by their mothers at birth were filling up the country's orphanages. Korean traditional society places significant weight on paternal family ties, bloodlines, and purity of race. Children of mixed race or those without fathers are not easily accepted in Korean society. Thousands were adopted by American families in the years

---

[9] People's Volunteer Army
[10] Korean People's Army

following the war, when their plight was covered on television. The U.S Immigration Act of 1952 removed race as a limiting factor in immigration, and made possible the entry of military spouses and children from South Korea after the Korean War. With the passage of the Immigration Act of 1965, which substantially changed U.S. immigration policy toward non-Europeans, Koreans became one of the fastest growing Asian groups in the United States.

Many volumes of study have focused on the fighting quality of U. S. forces in Korea during the war. The results of the study were mixed. While some units were praised for their fighting effectiveness there were many criticisms about units that were poorly led, trained, equipped, and suffered from low morale. Pork Chop Hill served as an excellent microseism for these conclusions. For example, many soldiers on Pork Chop Hill were killed not at their assigned guard or sentry positions but instead in their sleeping bags.

I had survived the heart of darkness that was Korea. I saw my first cousin carried away on a stretcher. I saw many men killed and have killed many men. I crawled through the human body parts and tissue. I will never forget the confused, angry and terrified face of the enemy Chinese soldier who almost bayoneted me, the white lieutenant who was killed just because he wanted to shake the coldness and cramps out of his legs. And I will never forget the cold and how it froze the dead and half dead faces of soldiers, friendly and enemy. These images haunt me to this day. I dream about my experiences frequently and during the day the images glide through my mind like faceless and frozen phantoms.

I've fulfill all my roles and responsibilities as an American soldier with honor and dignity in Korea for which I am proud. For my service in Korea I was awarded the Combat Infantry Badge[11], the United Nations Service Ribbon and the Korean Service Ribbon. Although young, I knew I was no longer a youngster, and now I was going home.

Long thought of as the "Forgotten War," by the American people, there is now a Korean War Memorial on the National Mall in Washington, DC, which was dedicated in July 1995. The memorial was built as an expression of the

---

[11] The Combat Infantryman Badge (CIB) is the U.S. Army combat service recognition decoration awarded to soldiers—enlisted men and officers (commissioned and warrant) holding colonel rank or below, who *personally* fought in active ground combat while an assigned member of either an infantry or a Special Forces unit, of brigade size or smaller, any time after 6 December 1941.

American people's gratitude to those who restored freedom to South Korea. Nineteen stainless steel sculptures stand silently under the watchful eye of a sea of faces upon a granite wall, reminders of the human cost of defending freedom. These elements all bear witness to the patriotism, devotion to duty, and courage of Korean War veterans.

Although I reside in the Washington metro area just minutes from the memorial, I have yet to visit it because the memories of the war and its tragedies are too fresh, and the pain too real even after 50 years. I don't think I will ever have the courage or strength to go.

CHAPTER 4

PEACETIME & MUCH ADO ABOUT NOTHING

My next duty station after Korea was an assignment with the 3rd Armored Cavalry Regiment based at Fort Meade, Maryland, where I was assigned from 1954 to 1957. I returned to the United States by ship which took 18 days to cross the pacific, finally docking in San Francisco. Travel by ship and the 18 days it took to reach the states was very therapeutic for me in that the time allowed me to decompress and become acclimated once again to the real world, unlike my return from Viet Nam many years later when no time to readjust before landing in the United States was available.   I then crossed by the country by train arriving in the Washington, DC and Fort Meade. Upon my arrival to Fort Meade I processed-in and was immediately given 30 days leave which I used to spend a considerable amount of time with my family and friends in South Carolina and elsewhere.

I was changed by my experiences in Korea, of course, how that could not be the case. I knew and felt physically, emotionally, and spiritually stronger as I now had more self-confidence, a strong sense of accomplishment from my personal achievements, feelings of euphoria for being one of the soldiers that survived, and came home physically unscathed. I wondered whether my family and friends would recognize the difference and whether they would still think of me as the "baby" in the family or now a man. When I returned to Aiken I was glad to see my mother and father, and my immediate family, as well as, the many young ladies about town.

It was good to be home, to be warm, wear regular shoes and clothes, see familiar faces, eat familiar foods, and away from the presence of fear, death, danger, and the smells of war. I also purchased another car, a 1940 Ford Fairlane, my previous car was a '38 Dodge Clarinet, with money I had saved while in Korea. With my mother I then traveled to Washington, DC, Philadelphia, and New York to revisit friends and family I had last seen one year earlier before deploying to Korea.

I've always traveled in public wearing my uniform. My uniform was a symbol of pride to show the public that I was a soldier in the United States Army and had served in combat. The uniform was also an indirect form of protection from random street or racial violence as I believed predators were less likely to assault a soldier who probably knew how to defend himself and kill if needed. I also wore my uniform, as all soldiers do, to impress the girls.

During my leave however, I had a strange sensation. Although I was glad to be home with my family and friends, I was also anxious to get back to Fort Meade and the army. In a way, Aiken was no longer my home and I was no longer the same young kid who had joined the army a year earlier. There were times when I felt anxious and wanted to leave but didn't because I knew it would upset my parents, particularly my mother. Years later, particularly after my service in Vietnam, I recognized that the anxiety I was having was related to post traumatic stress. I also did not leave Aiken at that time because I started a relationship with a young woman from town.

I returned to Fort Meade and reported for duty at the conclusion of my leave. In those days, the 3rd Armored

Cavalry had three battalions, the 1st and 2nd which were previously all white, and the 3rd which was all black. To my surprise I was assigned to Company A of the previously all white 1st Battalion. My platoon sergeant was Master Sergeant (MSG)) Montelongo (sp.) who was a Native American. The company 1st Sergeant was 1st Sergeant Burke. Both of these men were outstanding soldiers who took me under their wings and mentored me during the time I was in their unit. It was also during this time that I had decided to reenlist and make the army my career.

My decision to stay in the army and make it a career was easy. First, I liked the army. I liked the job, the responsibility, and the satisfaction I got for being a leader of infantry soldiers. As a squad leader in Korea I cared about my men and at times placed their welfare above my own. It is true and understandable that there is a special relationship and camaraderie among and between soldiers who serve in combat together that at times is equivalent to love. Also, as a soldier, you feel that you are doing something important on behalf of your government and humanity. For, example, soldiers are implementations of foreign policies made by government leaders and the work carried out by men in arms has a profound implication for the well-being of nations and its people. For example, had the United States and the UN not intervene in Korea, the South Koreans would have been enslaved under the communist system. Were it not for soldiers the world would have been a very different place had Japan and Germany won World War Two.

I also liked the army because I was good at what I did as evidenced by several rapid promotions I had received. In less than a year I had advanced from a Civilian to the rank of Sergeant and a squad leader. For all its faults, the army did have an equitable system for recognizing soldiers who excelled (and for those who don't) and give them the appropriate recognition through promotions, additional training, and assignment to leadership positions. I also like the notion that soldiers tend to look after each other and in some circumstances are willing to give their lives for their fellow soldiers.

Throughout our military history there have been numerous examples of soldiers who undertake extraordinary actions often sacrificing their own lives to save their fellow soldiers. For example, the roll of Medal of Honor recipients is replete with men who fell on hand grenades in foxholes to shield the explosion from other men; held gun positions alone holding back the enemy to allow other soldiers to retreat to safety; medics answering calls for help while under heavy fire from enemy guns and often losing their lives in the process, and many others examples of men making the ultimate sacrifice solely for helping other soldiers. One rarely sees example of similar kinds of heroic and sacrificial acts in the civilian world.

Due to my military record of achievement and professional attitude, I was given a special assignment by my new company 1st Sergeant. My duty was to track and keep a record of the company's daily activities, schedules, routines, and personnel which could then be easily retrieved and reviewed if necessary. Consequently, under the new tracking system the company commander or a visitor can request from me the daily tracking report, which I kept on a clipboard and immediately ascertain the status of all activities and personnel for that day. The procedure administered and managed by me was so effective, that it soon implemented throughout the squadron, much to the chagrin of the officers and NCOs of other units.

Throughout the history of the army men have joined and stayed in the military because of lack of economic opportunities in the civilian world. The army and the other military forces have always offered men and women meaningful and responsible jobs, training, positions of leadership and authority, pay and benefits that they could not get otherwise, especially in the civilian world. Career opportunities in the military were even more attractive for African Americans and other minorities who faced additional obstacles to receiving equal treatment and opportunities for jobs because of their race. The military was one of a only a few institutions in the United States that provided equal treatment and opportunities irrespective of race, which I've come to appreciate and was a key factor in my decision to remain in the army.

Similarly, in addition to the army providing equal opportunities for African Americans and other minorities, the army was also at the forefront of achieving racial integration years and even decades before the rest of the American society. While many parts of the American society was still heavily segregated in the mid-1950s with Jim Crow laws still on the books and enforced to ensure the supremacy of whites over African Americans, the army and the other armed services were aggressively moving forward to integrate its ranks and its community. Consequently, while the process had been slow, the military has progressively moved forward to achieve fairness and equality in the areas of promotions, assignment to leadership positions, training, housing, recreational facilities, schools, churches, clubs and organizations, and other aspects of the military community.

It was ironic to see for example the juxtaposition of military posts in the south that had fully integrated surrounded by communities that were still deeply segregated. It was like living in two worlds. I liked the fact the army was moving to change its society and community for the ultimate betterment of me and my family.

After making the decision to remain in the army I had set for myself a goal to someday to achieve the rank of 1st Sergeant. I decided that I wanted to become a 1st Sergeant because in those days, as now, 1st Sergeant was one of two of the highest enlisted rank in the army. Consequently, if you reached that rank you were at the top of the army's enlisted hierarchy and considered a significant personal and professional achievement. Next, I saw that 1st Sergeants occupied a unique position that commanded special reverence and respect that was different from those given to other ranks. As the "top" soldier in a company, it was the 1st

Sergeant who "ran" the company although it was the company commander who was in charge. I was also influenced to set this goal by several 1st Sergeants I had come to know and served with. These were men of honesty and integrity, who cared for the men under their charge. That was the kind of soldier and leader I wanted to be. In essence, I wanted to like them.

Up to now I had been in the infantry branch of the army, that is, I was a "foot" soldiers that did a lot of "walking" as part of my job. With my assignment with the 3rd Armored Cavalry I come to appreciate the power and flexibility of armored vehicles in war and the armored branch, and I especially like the idea that as a tanker I could now "ride" into combat instead of walking. To receive further training in armor, I was reassigned to Fort Knox, Kentucky, which at the time was the home of the armor school and armor branch.

At Fort Knox, a sprawling base of approximately 20,000 near Louisville, Kentucky, where I was assigned from 1957 to 1961, I received nine weeks of advanced armor training in the operations, maintenance, and capabilities of all armored and tracked vehicles in the army inventories. Vehicles I trained and worked on included the M41 and M48 main battle tanks. We had classes and training six days a week. I especially liked the live fire exercises using the main gun of the M48 tank. While at Fort Knox I had numerous other duties including tank commander with overall supervisory responsibility for three other men and operation of the tank; training NCO for a BCT unit for 18 months and finally I was assigned to an instructional committee responsible for developing lesson plans and training methods.

Operation Sage Brush was a major army field exercise I participated in while stationed at Fort Knox. The exercise was held in and around Fort Polk, Louisiana. It was a miserable assignment. Although I liked using the various tracked vehicle I was assigned, I hated the hot humid weather, the biting blood sucking insects, and of the four poisonous snakes we have in the United States, all of them can be found in Louisiana, especially at Fort Polk. During the entire exercise, I refused to bivouac or camp on the ground at night, instead choosing to sleep in or on my tank. I disliked my experiences in Louisiana so much that years later I extended, on two occasions, my tours in Vietnam rather than be reassigned to that base.

It was also during this period at Fort Knox that I came into contact with and had firsthand knowledge of the workings of the Woman Army Corps (WAC)[12]. Women have always served in the military during the 20th Century, but under certain restrictions. For example, unlike today, up until the early 1970s, women who became pregnant while unmarried had to be discharged from the service; nor hold certain jobs or MOSs. In essence, in their own way woman serving in the military had their own form of segregation. I believe one of the saddest facts of life for women serving in the military is the unfair and unearned stereotypes assigned to them about their virtues, sexual orientations, and motivation for being in the military. Some of the most beautiful and best women I have ever known were soldiers and I am proud to call them my own.

In addition to being outstanding woman and soldiers there were some who were also the funniest I have ever met. Such was the case of a female 1st Sergeant of a WAC unit whose barracks was located next to mine. She was a woman with the face that looked like Sammy Davis, Jr. and had the foulest and most humorous month I had ever heard. She could out curse a sailor in a single breath. For example,

---

[12] Women's Army Corps

it was customary to prepare barracks for inspection before being release for weekend passes. This 1st Sergeant was having difficulty motivating and getting her women to clean the barracks and was becoming frustrated in the process. So her pep talk to get the women motivated enough to perform their task was the most stirring and profound profanity laced speech I had ever heard. So much so it would have made a sailor cringe. My own modesty and sense of decorum prevents me from including this sergeant's exact words in this book, but, if the reader really wants to know what was said, please contact me at your convenience and I will be happy to tell you. In the end, the 1st Sergeant must have known how to motivate her troops because to my surprise, the women had the barracks cleaned in no time.

Although women have served honorably in America's military since 1901, gays on the other hand have always had a presence in the military, and as with women, they also served under certain constraints. Until 2011, it was illegal for gays to serve in any of the armed services, although it is estimated that approximately 20% of all military personnel are gay. Gays who served and those who are currently serving faced trail by court martial and discharged from service in some cases with less than honorable conditions.

Thus, gays who did serve and who are currently serving are forced to keep their sexual orientation and preferences hidden and forced to live secret lives.

Yet, despite the lack of official tolerance for gays by the military hierarchy, I found there is far greater tolerance for gay men and women by the rank and file of the army and the military, including myself. I have know many gays in the army and found them to be good soldiers, patriotic, and perform their duties with high proficiency. I believe that the tolerance for gays in the military by persons like myself is due also, in part, because they are seen as another minority group that has been subject to harsh discrimination and persecution by the majority. Thus, by supporting their rights we are also promoting our rights as African Americans and the rights of other minority groups.[13]

Although asked many times, I never considered serving in the army as a commissioned officer. Once in 1967, I turned down an opportunity to attend the army's officers' candidate school (OCS) which when completed I would have received a commission as a Second Lieutenant.

---

[13] The repeal of the Don't Ask Don't Tell policy was a de facto measure that now allows gays to serve openly in the military.

During the early parts of my army career I had little or no contact with African American officers who made up less than 3% of the officer corps. It was rare to see them and rarer still to know one personally. Perhaps if I had been mentored by officers as I had been by senior NCOs, the notion of becoming an officer would have been more viable. But, there were little opportunities or expectations for having that kind of relationship between an officer and an enlisted person at that time. Had I, perhaps my career in the army would have been different.

After about a year in the tank company, a request came down for experienced commissioned officers and NCOs with infantry experience to serve in a BCT unit. I volunteered and once assigned with the unit I was appointed the assistant platoon sergeant under a NCO named Sergeant First Class (SFC) Toth who was a fine soldier and gentleman. After about six months, I was asked to join an instructors' committee assigned to provide tactical and field exercise training. It was an excellent experience to serve on the committee because it gave me the opportunity to attend night classes and to add to my educational credentials for advancement in the army. Overall, during my time in the military, I attended three colleges with the aim of gaining knowledge, for its own sake, and to become more competitive when being considered for advancement and promotions in my career. After about a year serving on the committee another unit was started to teach armored communications. I was one of four NCO instructors selected to serve on the committee which taught classes during the day, which, again, allowed me to go school at night to further my formal education.

My neighbor at Fort Knox was Bill White who had played professional baseball under the New York Giants farm system. Most people only knew Bill through his affiliation with baseball, but I got to know him personally and we became well acquainted. He was a fine young man, however, due to differences in our ranks, I a sergeant and he a private, we did not socialize that much. Another friend of mine was Stanley "Jazz Man" Turnitune. Stanley was a great jazz horn blower who was a member of the army band. We remain great friends even after he left the army. We met again many years later in Maryland.

After nearly four years at Fort Knox, I received order assigning me to Germany. I enjoyed my life and experiences at Fort Knox, including the colleges courses I took at night, but I was anxious go to Europe and begin the next phase of my military career.

I reported to the 4TH Infantry, 37th Armored at Schweinfurt, Germany in 1961, located approximately near the geographical center of modern day Germany. In 1961 when I reported for duty, Schweinfurt was near the border that separated East and West Germany and the very hot and contentious frontline of the cold war. I was assigned to the headquarters Platoon of B Company, 37th Armored Cavalry Regiment of the 4th Infantry. I was attached to the Headquarters Battalion Tank Section for my first two years and was fortunate to have, as in my previous units, a very supportive and encouraging company 1st Sergeant from Kentucky, 1st Sergeant Ernest E. Cowles, who also served as my mentor. We saw each other on a daily basis since we were quartered in the same barracks. We spent a lot of time talking about the army. He explained to me how to set up an orderly room and which army manuals and written regulations were necessary to have. He showed me how to prepare duty rosters and morning reports and most importantly how to treat men with honesty, integrity, and respect. I saw and learned from him how to get the best out of men. I was eventually reassigned to the headquarters platoon and made assistant platoon sergeant. But, I wanted more time with a regular line platoon so I asked and was granted my request which helped to further my military education and experience level.

Because I was one of several senior NCOs living in the barracks, I had gotten to know personally many men who otherwise I would not have gotten to met had I lived off base. One of the men I met was a young soldier who was the grandson of the movie mogul Cecil B. DeMille. This soldier was also the nephew of actor Anthony Quinn.

In addition to my duties, I also had training in the German language provided by the army and went to demolition school. In 1961, I received another promotion to Staff Sergeant (SSG), E6.

My unit's primary mission was to train and be prepared for war with the Soviet Union. My unit was constantly in the field on maneuvers and conducted live-fire exercises in the German country side. Our other mission was to provide security for mobile missiles launchers and cannons that fired atomic and nuclear tipped projectiles.

The most notable event during my tour in Germany was the Cuban Missiles Crisis of 1961 in which the Soviet Union and the United States nearly went to war over Russian missiles based on the Caribbean island of Cuban located about 90 miles from Florida. From my perspective stationed in Germany, if war came it would happen first in Germany with tanks and men of the Warsaw Pact charging into Western Europe against the American and NATO forces. It didn't occur to me at all the fight between the two countries could possibly include direct nuclear exchanges against each respective country.

My unit and all other units of the American army and NATO forces were on full alert which placed us in or near our tanks and other equipment prepared for action had war came. The wait for the next step and the uncertainty caused a great deal of anxiety and concern for all of us. By October, 1961, much to my relief, the crisis had been averted and we were order to stand down.

In February 1963, I received orders reassigning me to the United States. When I arrived at Fort Hamilton, New York with my wife, who met me there, we were told there was no available temporary lodging for us on base but an effort would be made to help find a hotel room. As it happened, a colonel stationed at Fort Hamilton heard about our plight and offered to give us a complimentary pass that allowed us to stay at the famed Waldorf Astoria Hotel on Park Avenue in New York City, which we gladly accepted. I never heard of any other enlisted military personnel having the opportunity to stay at the Waldorf. Of course, this storied and historic hotel which was the full-time resident of General of Army Douglas MacArthur at the same time we were there, was wonderful. In addition to a great room, whose number I still remember: Room 1805, we were treated to a steak dinner at its famous restaurant. I recall the waiter giving us a 15 minute speech about the history and quality of the steak we were about to eat.

After reporting to Fort Hamilton, I received a 30 day leave which I spent with the wife, children, and parents. After my leave I received order to report to the 5th Mechanized Infantry Division at Fort Irwin located in the dessert regions of southern California for dessert warfare and weapons training, and where I would be stationed for the next one and a half years.

Serving in California was a great experience which offered many exciting and entertainment opportunities off base. Once after I had completed a special assignment and while having dinner at the Coconut Grove in Los Angeles, I was approached by an attractive woman who introduced herself and said she noticed the 7th Infantry Division patch on the right shoulder of my uniform. She said her father had served with the 7th Infantry in Korea where he was killed. She wanted to know if I had known him. I said I didn't. As it happened, the women and her friends were friends of the popular African American singer Nancy Wilson, to whom she later introduced me to and I took pictures with. Additionally, the same women also introduced me to her mother who was actor Tony Curtis' house maid. On several occasions when Curtis was away, she would invite my wife, our kids, and me to his house in Palm Springs which was amazing to see.

During this time, I also met a guy named Roland Kirk who was born blind but still finished college at Ohio State University. Despite his handicap he was able to the blow three different horns at the same time producing excellent music. At another time, I met Emmitt Ashford who was the first African American umpire in professional baseball.

During the off season he sold cars and I purchased a new Pontiac from him.

While at Fort Irwin I had the opportunity to participate in a nine week field exercise in the state of Washington with the U S Army Special Forces, Green Berets. To prepare for the exercise we did a lot of mountain climbing and running to get in shape. I made a lot of good friends in the Special Forces during the exercise and we stayed in contact long afterwards. Following the field exercise with the green berets, I attended school for chemical, biological and radiological warfare at Fort McClellan, Alabama. When I arrived for training I was told I would be in charge of the class because I was senior in rank. The NCOIC[14] told me not to worry about my shorter time in service, relative to others in the class, and that I will do just fine.

Summer months in the California dessert was very hot. To escape the heat we often trained early in the morning, sometimes before day break, between 4 am – 10 am, and later in the afternoon or at night. To get out of the heat we often crawl under rocks as did the snakes, lizards, scorpions, and other critters of the dessert. California was

---

[14] Noncommissioned officer in charge,

nice but I was becoming restless and thought it was time for me to move on to my next assignment and to other adventures.

It was at Fort Irwin in 1964 that I first heard someone mentioned the word "Vietnam." It was when a fellow soldier had just returned from the army's language school at Monterey, California where he attended the Vietnamese language course. The next time I heard someone mention Vietnam was on a television show. The show was Route 66. The show's stars were Marty Milner and George Maharis. The dramatic series was about two young men that traveled throughout country along the now famed Route 66; solving problems for people they met while they themselves were coming of age.

When the new season for the show started George Maharis had left the series and his character was replaced by Glen Corbett, who played a sensitive, brooding, and somewhat troubled army veteran who was a former green beret or special forces soldier that had just returned from a place called "Vietnam." Like myself, few Americans if any could have known about the existence of the place called Vietnam when the show aired and fewer still, including myself, could have know the about the role that country would play in our history, and in my life, in matter of a few short months.

Whether I did it for career advancement, ambition, adventure, or to escape the boredom of the peacetime army, or for reasons I may never know, I volunteered to also take the Vietnamese language course and for service in Vietnam.

My Grandmother & Grandfather, on my mother's side,
Tom and Lizzy Thomas.

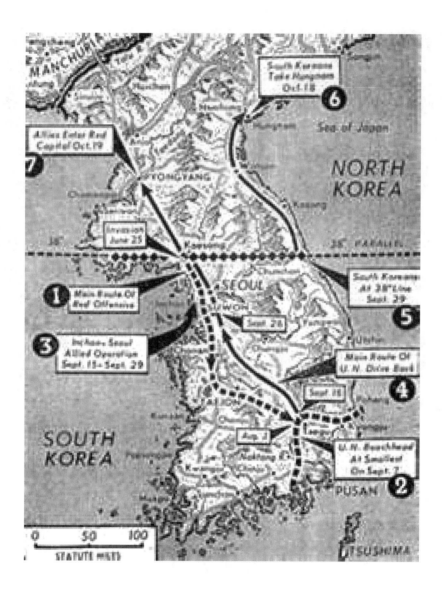

Korea, Circa 1950

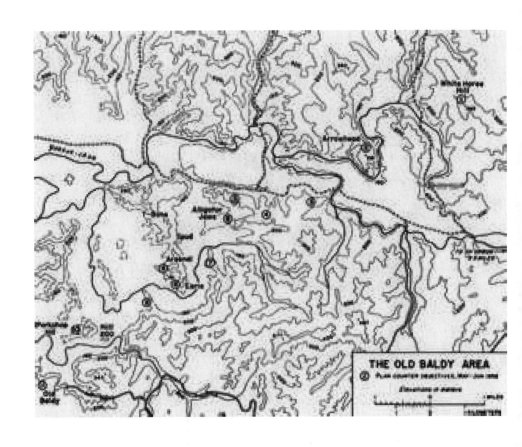

Aerial View of Pork Chop Hill

Trench on Pork Chop Hill

Entrance to a Bunker

Wounded being evacuated from a bunker

Roof of bunker being reinforced with wooden beam

Me and my beautiful 1940 Ford Fairlane at Fort Meade, 1954

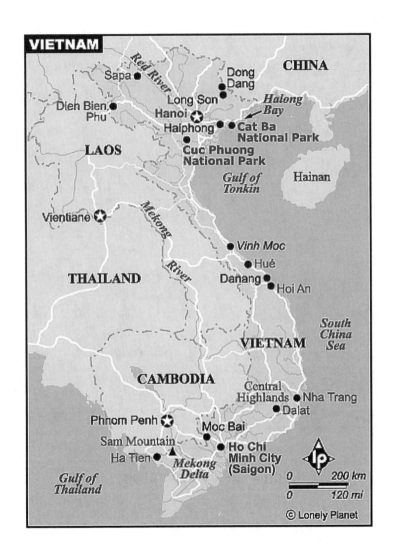

Indochina

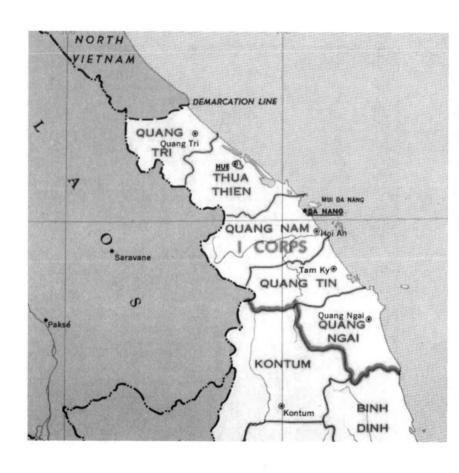

I Corps Area of Operation

War Zone D

MACV Advisor with ARVN counterpart, 1964/1965

MACV Advisor with ARVN counterpart, 1964/1965

Me at rifle range with ARVN troops. Note shiny boots.

1964/1965

Me with fellow tankers of 4th Cavalry, 1st Infantry, 1967/1968

Me in front of the M48 Tank, 4th Cavalry, 1st Infantry Division, 1967/1968

Me in back of the M48 Tank, 4th Cavalry, 1st Infantry Division, 1967/1968

MACV Advisor, 1964/1965

Me with 50 Caliber machinegun, 4th Cavalry, 1st Infantry
Division, 1967/1968

MACV Advisor, 1964/1965

MACV Advisor, 1964/1965

Many good soldiers lost in Vietnam

M113 APC

Me on top of tank, 4th Cavalry, 1st Infantry Division, 1967/1968

1st Sergeant of all female AIT unit at Fort Jackson

M48 Main Battle Tank

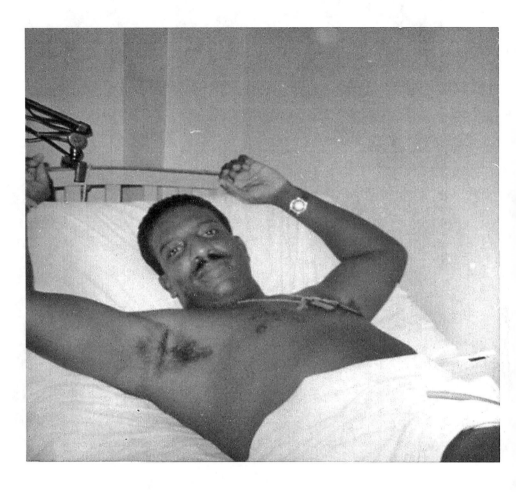

Recovering at Walter Reed Army Hospital

Received recognition for Superior Performance, Fort
Myers, 1968

1st Sergeant, U S Army Headquarters Company, Fort Myers, 1969/1970

Photo Taken for Sergeant Major Promotion Board,
1970/1971

My wife Esther Stroy during her competitive track days

My wife, Esther Story, and I on our wedding day

CHAPTER 5

VIETNAM & PUTTING FIRE WITH GASOLINE

I arrived in Vietnam by commercial flight in April 1964 after departing from Fort Ord, California. After a two week orientation training to learn about the history and customs of the country, I was assigned to the Military Assistance Command – Vietnam (MCAV) Advisory Team in the I Corps region of South Vietnam. Vietnam's military regions were divided by sections called Corps numbering from I to IV. I Corps was located in the northern most region of the country and the IV Corps was in the south. Headquarters for MACV Advisory Team for I Corp was in Da Nang located on the northern coast. The advisory team for each region or corps was divided into individual groups or sub-teams consisting of one officer and two enlisted men who would in turn be assigned to individual Vietnamese army units as military advisory.

By the time I arrived in-country, Vietnam had already been fighting for a long time. Between 1945 and 1954, the Vietnamese waged an anti-colonial war against France and received financial support from the United States. The French defeat at the Dien Bien Phu was followed by a peace conference in Geneva, in which Laos, Cambodia, and Vietnam received their independence and Vietnam was temporarily divided between an anti-Communist South and a Communist North. In 1956, South Vietnam, with American backing, refused to hold the unification elections. By 1958, Communist-led guerrillas known as the Viet Cong had begun to battle the South Vietnamese government.

To support the South's government, the United States sent in 2,000 military advisors, a number that grew to 16,300 by 1963. The military condition deteriorated, and by 1963 South Vietnam had lost the fertile Mekong Delta to the Vietcong. By 1964 Vietnam was at precipice. Should the United States send more troops to support the South Vietnamese government or should we cut our losses and withdraw. We choose the former.

American military advisors have served in Vietnam since World War II, albeit in very small numbers. The advisers who served in Indochina and Vietnam first were political, economic, and military advisers to the French, who returned to Indochina at the end of World War II. Our involvement was largely economic in nature and we moved gradually, during the Truman and Eisenhower administrations, toward deeper commitments. American military aid reached $2.5 billion between 1950 and 1954.

The chief means of our involvement, during the First Indochina War, was through the advisory apparatus known as Military Assistance and Advisory Group (MAAG), first known as MAAG Indochina, and through the military's volunteer forces known as Special Forces. All involved were "advisers" rather than combat troops. Along with political, diplomatic, and economic advisers, these advised the French in their war against the Vietnamese, known as the First Indochina War.

No example of our advisory role before 1961, however, is better than the military training of South Vietnam's own Special Forces. The mission of the first American Special Forces in Vietnam was to train fewer than one hundred Vietnamese soldiers. The first training center was in Nha Trang. The Americans arrived from Okinawa in the summer of 1957, and by 1960 they were training more than fifty Ranger units of the Army of the Republic of

Vietnam (ARVN). Although this aspect of the advisory experience began in the Eisenhower presidency, it was greatly expanded under the keen interest and direction of President Kennedy later.

After the French left, and prior to Kennedy's inauguration, the U.S. role expanded due to several considerations. Defending the Republic of Vietnam became a direct burden of the U.S. It became a battle within the Cold War. Eisenhower, a great believer in the domino theory, led the nation into new commitments -- training of counterinsurgency Vietnamese troops, nation-building efforts on a broad scale, and the placement of our nation's largest diplomatic corps in Saigon. We assisted the southern Vietnamese in a battle for the "hearts and minds" of the people by means of a Strategic Hamlet Program. In addition, we pumped more and more foreign and military aid into South Vietnam.

However, under Eisenhower, we avoided a wider war in 1953-54, and our deepening commitments remained limited in contrast to later escalations under both presidents Kennedy and Johnson. We may have had more than 1,500 Americans in South Vietnam by 1961, and our Saigon mission was the largest in the world. MAAG's strength, however, had increased to only 692 persons. Nevertheless, this was a violation of the Geneva Accord limitation to 342 advisers.

MACV was created on February 8, 1962, in response to the increase in U.S. military assistance to South Vietnam. MACV was first implemented to assist the Military Assistance Advisory Group (MAAG) Vietnam, controlling every advisory and assistance effort in Vietnam, but was reorganized in 1964 and absorbed MAAG Vietnam to its command when combat unit deployment became too large for advisory group control.

I was one of a three man advisory team that consisted of an officer, Captain Smith an infantry officer, and two enlisted men, me and Sergeant Hicks. We were assigned to be advisors to the elite 11th Ranger Battalion in the I Corps region of northern South Vietnam. The ranger battalion, which consisted of approximately 43 officers and 600 men, had its base camp in the jungle approximately 75 miles from it actual headquarters in Da Nang. Like most elite units, all of the members of the battalion were volunteers that underwent rigorous training in commando and guerilla warfare and tactics. The rangers were highly motivated to carry the fight to the enemy on any given day, but only under the right conditions.

The primary role of American military advisors during that period of the war was to provide Vietnamese unit commanders advice related to tactics, strategy, training, intelligence, psychological warfare, communications, civil affairs, medical assistance, and encouragement. Our role was purely advisory and Americans were not expected to play an active role in actual combat against the Viet Cong or North Vietnamese forces. Further, acceptance of "advice" from Americans was largely voluntary and Vietnamese officers were not required to follow the advice given.

There was definitely a cultural clash between American advisors and Vietnamese military commanders and soldiers with respect to how wars are viewed and should be fought. For example, although the base camp of the ranger battalion, where most of the men were, was located in the field often surrounded by hostile enemy forces, the senior officers and commander of the unit made their headquarters and personal living quarters far away in the relative comfort and safety of Da Nang.

Another example of the differences between American and Vietnamese tactical views and war fighting philosophy was the tendency by Vietnamese commanders to break off contact with the enemy after a fight has begun or not pursue the enemy to continue the battle if they, the enemy, was in retreat. I have witnessed many instances when the ranger unit could have achieved a decisive victory had they remain persistent and continue the attack against the enemy unit.

The lack of aggressiveness by Vietnamese should not be viewed as an act of cowardliness nor their reluctance to fight. I would contend that most Vietnamese officers were competent commanders. What seem to have contributed to the Vietnamese officers' peculiar perspective on war was the French influenced. At that time most senior level Vietnamese officers had been trained by the French who had instilled in them that these kinds of military tactics and attitudes about war were acceptable and legitimate.

The primary mission of the 11th Ranger Battalion was to conduct search and destroy missions in their sector and provide protection for the development of the Da Nang airbase in preparation of the arrival of U. S. Marines by 1965. The battalion to which I was assigned conducted almost daily search and destroy mission in our sector. A typical day started with reveille which was at day break, followed by breakfast and briefing. Troops would then be loaded unto helicopters, Huey UH-1 and Chinooks, and flown to villages, hamlets, farms, hillsides or anywhere it was suspected the Viet Cong were. Helicopters would typically land a little distance from a site to be searched and some of the troops would set up a perimeter around the village for security while others would enter and begin to conduct a search for individuals in hiding who may be Viet Cong or for weapons and other contrabands. While the search was being conducted intelligence officers may begin to interrogate various individuals for information, often under the threat of violence.

If weapons or suspected Viet Cong were found there would be immediate reprisals. The village could be burned and its food supply destroyed under the assumption that the people in the village must be providing support for the Viet Cong. Any suspected Viet Cong would be taken prisoner and transported back to base camp for further, often harsh interrogation. When Vietnamese soldiers began burning huts and other structures and destroying the food needed by the people, the wail created by crying women and children was chilling and haunting. Although it seemed legitimate to take the action we did then, in retrospect these actions were the seeds that will eventually lead to the beginning of the end for the possibility of a military victory in Vietnam. It was like putting out a fire with gasoline.

Each advisory sub-team such as the one I was assigned was reassigned after serving six months with a particular unit. When my six months ended with the 11th Ranger Battalion I was reassigned to the Vietnamese 4th Armored Cavalry Regiment based in Tam Kie, a city that was in the same I Corps region. I was assigned to the 4th Cavalry because of my armor and track vehicle experience prior to coming to Vietnam. My new counterpart was First Lieutenant (1LT) Templeton[15] who had also been in the country the previous six months with another unit. He was an excellent officer and we spent a lot of time together during the course of the assignment.

The frequency and intensity of the contacts and battles, and the size of enemy forces increased significantly during my assignment with the 4rd Cavalry. As with the 11th Ranger Battalion, my new unit went out on frequently search and destroys missions and provided armored support for

---

[15] Templeton was a son of a Hollywood filmmaker. His obituary is provided as Appendix E, page 228.

Vietnamese infantry units. It was during this period that I began to detect a shift in the attitudes and tactical behavior of Vietnamese commanders in how they fight. The change may be attributed to an increase in the learning curve by Vietnamese commanders on battlefield tactics, the training of Vietnamese officers and NCOs in the United States, and the ever larger presence of American advisor in-country to help their counterparts in war fighting. The other possibility I considered was that the Viet Cong was themselves becoming better fighters, consequently, the South Vietnamese had to adjust their behavior and tactics accordingly in order to meet the new challenge.

Evidence of the new attitudes and tactics was provided in July 1964 when we received reports that a large Viet Cong force of over 2000 men had dug-in and created a defensive line not far from our base camp, Tam Kie. One battalion of the Vietnamese 4th Cavalry of approximately 1500 men with their armored vehicles were ordered to move toward and destroy the enemy. This battle lasted three days and resulted in heavy causalities on both sides. Our unit arrived and got into position the night before the battle on the first day. Our defensive line extended beyond those of the VCs to prevent any flanking movement or attacks. By day break, both defensive lines were established and were approximately 300-500 yards apart. The Viet Cong distinctive black pajama type uniforms could be easily seen from our position.

The enemy, their approximate numbers, and their positions were clearly visible from where we were. The battle began at approximately 8:30 am when the troops of the 4th Cavalry began their forward movement towards the enemy lines. The air erupted with small arms fire, mortars rounds, heavy machineguns, and the big guns of the tanks. I could see we were taking heavy causalities as men began falling on the ground as they were hit by gunfire or torn to pieces by mortars. The fighting was very intense and throughout the day it was clear we were making very little progress toward the VC's emplacement. As day turned to night we broke contact and retreated back to our base camp leaving the dead and wounded for collection the next day.

We returned on the second day to continue the fight with reinforcements and additional firepower and air support. We were once again in approximately the same defensive positions as the previous day. Again, at approximately 8:30 am we began the attack, but this time with determination and ferocity, and with greater firepower. As the troops advanced forward they passed bodies of those killed the previous day and saw that the bodies had been mutilated by the VCs. Some of the bodies had the skins of their faces flayed back over the top of the head revealing the skull. Other bodies showed evidence that their penises had been severed. The sight was grisly but it seems to provide our men with extra determination to kill the enemy and win the battle. As the day progressed it was clear that our troops were winning the battle with the help of additional manpower and troops we put into the fight, and the artillery and air support that pounded the VCs. By the end of the second day, we had completely over run all of their positions, killing many men. The third day of the battle was devoted to clearing the surrounding area of any remaining VCs and collecting the dead and wounded. Causalities on both sides were very high. I estimate over 700 VCs were killed and we had lost approximately 150 men.

Mistreatment against civilians and prisoners happens in all wars and the VCs committed terrible atrocities. I saw numerous instances of VC murdering men, women, and children in order to instill fear and achieve their military or political aims. In some villages the VCs often hacked bodies into pieces and placed the parts in a circle around a flag pole where the flag of South Vietnam once flew. Civilians were summarily executed without reason or notice.

But, these kinds of atrocities happen both ways. One South Vietnamese Master Sergeant who was a Montayard, a distinct ethnic group found in Vietnam's central highlands had a tendency to cut hearts out of the chests of living VC captives and roast the meat over the exhaust of vehicles. When he thought the heart was sufficiently cooked he would eat it. This soldier told us did this because the VC had killed and mutilated his entire family and this was his form of revenge. When I told my team leader Captain Gary Templeton about these incidents, at first he didn't believe it, but when he saw it happen for the first time he emptied the full contents of his stomach.

As my one year tour in Vietnam was about to end I received orders that I would be reassigned to a BCT unit at dreaded Fort Polk, Louisiana for my next duty station. Remembering my experiences with Operation Sage Brush in 1958 with all the snakes, insects, and heat of Louisiana, I offered to extend my tour in Vietnam for another six months to avoid being sent to Fort Polk. Somehow I reasoned that war and all its horror was better than being in Louisiana.

When my request for extension was approved I was pulled out of the field and assigned to a Vietnamese training center just outside of Da Nang. It was a good duty assignment as my new responsibilities was to provide instructions to Vietnamese soldiers on infantry tactics and operations. I had my own living quarters, jeep, interpreter, and was for the moment out of harms way. I really had it made.

As my final tour was about to end I began to reflect on my experiences in the country. First, I was pleased with my overall performance as a military advisor and with my personal behavior, conduct, and valor while under fire in combat. However, I was uncertain as to what the outcome of the war might be. I thought, however, if we were to win this war we needed more advisors. But, I never imagine then that at one point more than 500,000 American servicemen would be stationed in Vietnam.

The awards I received for my duty in Vietnam was a second Combat Infantry Badge, Bronze Star[16] with "V"[17] Device for Valor, and two Vietnamese Cross for Gallantry

---

[16] The Bronze Star Medal (or BSM) is a United States Armed Forces individual military decoration that may be awarded for bravery, acts of merit, or meritorious service. When awarded for bravery, it is the fourth-highest combat award of the U.S. Armed Forces and the ninth highest military award
[17] "V" denotes valor or bravery.

with Palm[18]. I also held the distinction of being the only military advisor to have served in three distinct capacities during my tour. I was an advisor with an infantry unit, an armored unit, and finally as an instructor. My next duty station was Vilseck, Germany with the Combined Armored School of the 3rd Armored Division. This time I was glad to go.

---

[18] The Vietnam Gallantry Cross was a military decoration of South Vietnam which was established in August 1950. Also known as the Vietnamese Cross of Gallantry, the Gallantry Cross was awarded to any military personnel who have accomplished deeds of valor or displayed heroic conduct while fighting an enemy force. It was modeled after the French Croix de guerre.

CHAPTER 6

GERMAN INTERLUDE

This assignment to Germany was different from the one in 1961 because I was able to bring my entire family with me and due to my rank of Staff Sergeant, I was guaranteed living quarters. I was assigned as an instructor on the weapons committee at the combat arms school located in Vilseck approximately 100 miles from Frankfurt. It was here, after more than 12 years in the army that I encountered my first significant incident of racism.

When I arrived at Vilseck but before I reported for duty I met a number of soldiers who expressed their concerns to me about my new supervisor and NCOIC (noncommissioned officer in charge) who had a reputation of not liking African Americans and giving African American and other minority soldiers a hard time. I listened but was not overly concerned because I knew I could handle these types of situations and felt it was always good to give everyone the benefit of the doubt, which I did. When I met my new supervisor, we had a pleasant conversation, but I noticed he was distant and appeared disinterested in me and in my assignment to the committee. I did not expect him to offer to mentor me as other senior NCOs had done who were my superiors. Prior to coming to German I had purchased a brand new car. My new supervisor questioned me about how I could afford a new car at my my rank and while having to support a family. He indicated that he was not able to purchase new car and wonder how I was able to. By the tone of his questioning I inferred that he was insinuating that the money I used to buy the car must have come from an illegal or illegitimate source. I explained to him, in an pretentious and condescending way, that a "smart" person, needs to be diligent with money and try to save every month, if only a few dollars. As an example, I told him about the allotment and joint bank account I had with my mother and sister from the start of my army career. I also explain to him that I didn't drink, smoke, gamble, or spend money on various vices, in such a way to suggest that maybe he did. He was unimpressed with my story and probably not very bright as he seemed to have missed completely the sarcasm on my part.

He then told me that my first duty assignment was to give a one hour lecture before a group of officers and NCOs on the proper use of a standard screw driver in five days. At first I was dismayed and then grew angry about the

144

assignment that was given to me. The topic and the purpose of the "lecture" were obviously juvenile and a waste of time. I believe he expected me to deliver a poor presentation and not cover the entire time allotted. But, I resolved to defeat him at his own game by giving a very professional and the best possible lecture anyone had ever heard on the use screw driver.

I began by collecting as many and as varied types of screw drivers as possible. I collected screw drivers of different sizes, shapes, and colors; I collected screw drivers that were powered, manual, and screw drivers with many different types of bits or points used on specific types of screw heads. I then prepared a formal lesson plan. On the day of the lecture the room was filled with officers and senior NCOs from my unit and on a number of dimensions I gave an outstanding and thorough lecture, for one full hour, on the use of the screw driver. When I concluded my talk the ranking officer in the room stood and said in front of everyone, "Sergeant Harper, I must say here and now that was the best lecture I have ever heard on any topic, congratulation!" In reply, while looking directly at my NCOIC who had given me the assignment, I said, "Sir, thank you. My only regret is that I didn't have more time to continue my lesson on the proper use of the screw driver."

I believe that it is a truism in the army that these kinds of tensions and animosities between soldiers rarely happens during war or in a combat zone, but they become more prevalent during peacetime when soldiers instead of fighting an enemy army, seek other diversions to fill their time by often fighting each other. That was evident just before I left Korea after the armistice had been signed. A soldier from Oakland, California had been harassing me for no other reason than I was a very young sergeant[19] that had performed exceptionally well during my tour in Korea. He finally challenged me to fist fight and, to his surprise, I kicked his rear beyond any shadow of doubt, and his harassment of me stopped.

Additionally, I believe soldiers that have had combat experience have difficulties adjusting to the everyday mundane aspects of life and families when they are not in war zones and in time grow restless and express their restlessness and frustrations in odd and often self-destructive ways. I feared during my assignment in Germany that I may be such a person.

---

[19] A buck sergeant is the junior most sergeant in the army. Buck refers to a buck deer or a "young" deer.

The terror, horror and the excitement of war never leaves men who have served in combat. How these thoughts and memories impact men are functions of how well adjusted mentally, emotionally, and spirituality they are and are not necessarily related to the severity of the combat experience. Indeed, thoughts of my near death experiences in Korea and Vietnam have always haunted me but I believe I have dealt with these issues well because of the spiritual and emotional training I received from my parents as well as from some internal source of my own whose origins I am unsure.

The experience and excitement of combat is like a drug addiction for some men. Some men cope with the addition by denying its existence and/or by channeling the confused emotional feeling about what to do with these feelings by drinking, drug abuse, violence, and undertaking other devious behavior. Other men deal with these feelings and issues by returning to combat. I may fall into the latter.

After my assignment was completed at the combat arms school I was assigned the assistant operations NCOIC for the 3rd Armored Division. One day, I received a call from an officer from the staff of Major General William DePuy, the commanding general of the 1st Infantry Division. I was told by the officer that the division, which was already deployed to Vietnam, was searching for hand-picked commissioned and noncommissioned officers to join the unit. Specifically, he said, General DePuy had heard about me and my record and that wanted to ask if I was interested in be assigned to the 1st Division. I thought to myself about how bored I was In Europe and how bored I was with my army life. I was a combat soldier. I was flattered to be asked and I said I would agree to go back to Vietnam and join the *Big Red 1*.

In most cases assignment of personnel to army units is made by some large bureaucratic machinery that seemingly make such assignments by chance or some other mysterious process. For the most part, that is how soldiers' assignments are made in the military. However, commanders also have the option to make requests for specific individuals to be assigned to their units and select those individuals whose performance as soldiers they are familiar with or select those who have skills and expertise they require. Consequently, commanders like to select their own subordinate unit commanders, other direct reports, and individuals they know will add value to their units and commands.

There was something else that I had noticed while stationed in Germany. The army and the world was in the mist of profound and dynamic social, cultural, and political changes brought by people like the Beatles, Martin Luther King, H Rap Brown, Stokely Carmichael, Abbie Hoffman, Russell Banks, John & Robert Kennedy, Dennis Means, Charlie Manson, the Hippies, African American Power Movement, just to name a few. The changes were all encompassing and included wars, internal conflicts, coups, nuclear threats, decolonization and independence, assassinations, natural disasters, amazing scientific and technological advances, social movements that included the counterculture, anti-war movement, feminism, civil rights movement, rising crime, and pop culture.

The period was called the 60s and denoted the complex of inter-related cultural and political trends across the globe. To some it was the era of irresponsible excess and flamboyance and marked by the relaxation of some social taboos especially relating to sexism and racism. And some saw the era as a classical nightmare cycle, where a rigid culture, unable to contain the demands for greater individual freedom, broke free of the social constraints of the previous age through extreme deviation from the norm.

149

Two prominent movements during the period were the counter-culture and the anti-Vietnam movements. In the second half of the decade, young people began to revolt against the conservative norms of the time, as well as remove themselves from mainstream liberalism, in particular the high level of materialism which was so common during the era. This created a "counterculture" that sparked a social revolution throughout much of the western world. It began in the United States as a reaction against the conservatism and social conformity of the 1950s, and the US government's extensive military intervention in Vietnam.

The youth involved in the popular social aspects of the movement became known as hippies. These groups created a movement toward liberation in society, including the sexual revolution, questioning authority and government, and demanding more freedoms and rights for women and minorities. The Underground Press, a widespread, eclectic collection of newspapers served as a unifying medium for the counterculture. The movement was also marked by the first widespread, socially accepted drug use (including LSD and marijuana) and psychedelic music.

The war in Vietnam would eventually lead to a commitment of over half a million American troops, resulting in over 58,500 American deaths and producing a large-scale antiwar movement in the United States. As late as the end of 1965, few Americans protested the American involvement in Vietnam, but as the war dragged on and the body count continued to climb, civil unrest escalated. Students became a powerful and disruptive force and university campuses sparked a national debate over the war. As the movement's ideals spread beyond college campuses, doubts about the war also began to appear within the administration itself. A mass movement began rising in opposition to the Vietnam War, ending in the massive Moratorium protests in 1969, as well as the movement of resistance to conscription ("the Draft") for the war.

The antiwar movement was initially based on the older 1950s Peace movement, but by the mid-1960s it outgrew this and became a broad-based mass movement centered in universities and churches: one kind of protest was called a "sit-in". Other terms heard in the United States included "the Draft", "draft dodger", "conscientious objector", and "Vietnam vet". Voter age-limits were challenged by the phrase: "If you're old enough to die for your country, you're old enough to vote." Many of the youth involved in the politics of the movements distanced themselves from the "hippies."

. In 1965, Johnson escalated the war, commencing air strikes on North Vietnam and committing ground forces, which numbered 536,000 in 1968. The 1968 Tet Offensive by the North Vietnamese turned many Americans against the war. America had changed and so had its attitude toward the Vietnam War, especially since my first tour in 1964.

In January, 1967 I packed-up my family and returned to the United States and took a 30-days leave. I repeated the process of saying goodbye to my family members and friends while getting my wife and family resettled in the Washington, DC area and then with little fanfare I was once again, gone!

CHAPTER 7

VIETNAM REDUX

From 1965 to 1968, we were involved in a limited war in Vietnam. Although there were aerial bombings of the North, President Johnson wanted the fighting to be limited to South Vietnam. By limiting the fighting parameters, the our forces would not conduct a serious ground assault into the North to attack the communists directly nor would there be any strong effort to disrupt the Ho Chi Minh Trail (the Viet Cong's supply path that ran through Laos and Cambodia).

We fought a jungle war, mostly against the well-supplied Viet Cong. The Viet Cong would attack in ambushes, set up booby traps, and escape through a complex network of underground tunnels. For us, even just finding their enemy proved difficult. Since Viet Cong hid in the dense brush, we would drop Agent Orange or napalm bombs which cleared an area by causing the leaves to drop off or to burn away. In every village, we had difficulty determining which, if any, villagers were the enemy since even women and children could build booby traps or help house and feed the Viet Cong. We often became frustrated with the fighting conditions in Vietnam. Many suffered from low morale, became angry, and some used drugs.

On January 30, 1967, the North Vietnamese surprised both us and the South Vietnamese by orchestrating a coordinated assault with the Viet Cong to attack about a hundred South Vietnamese cities and towns. Although we and the South Vietnamese army were able to repel the assault known as the Tet Offensive, this attack proved to Americans that the enemy was stronger and better organized than they had been led to believe. The Tet Offensive was a turning point in the war because President Johnson, faced now with an unhappy American public and bad news from his military leaders in Vietnam, decided to no longer escalate the war.

When I arrived in Vietnam in January 1967, the nation and the war boiling within it was a very different place from the one I had seen during my first tour as an advisor in 1964. The massive military buildup was evident everywhere as the number of United States' forces grew from a several thousand military advisors in 1964 to nearly 500,000 in 1968.

I was assigned to Troop C, 4th Armored Cavalry Squadron, also known as the Quarter Horse Squadron, of the 1st Infantry Division, based at Fu Loy, 30 miles from Da Nang. The motto of the 1st Infantry Division is, "If you are going to be One, Be the Big Red One." Because the platoon I was assigned to didn't have a platoon leader who was typically an officer and a lieutenant, I was told I would also serve as the acting platoon leader until a replacement could be found. My platoon consisted of 44 men of which about a third were African Americans and Hispanics and the rest white. The platoon had assigned to it ten track vehicles, three M48A1 tanks and seven M113 APCs.

I was lucky in a sense to be assigned to the 1st Infantry and the 4th cavalry because they had a reputation for being outstanding units lead by the best officers in the army. The Division's history begins in 1917 when General John "Blackjack" Pershing arrived in France with the First American Expeditionary Force. The "Fighting First" led the way for American troops in World War I. Names like Cantigny, Soissons, St. Mihiel and the Argonne Forest tell the story of the gallantry of the soldiers of the 1st Infantry Division, now wearing the famous "Big Red One" patch on their left shoulder.

During World War II, the 1st Infantry Division was the first to reach England, the first to fight the enemy in North Africa and Sicily, the first on the beaches of Normandy in D-Day and the first to capture a major German City – Aachen.

The D-Day landings on June 6, 1944 provided the supreme test. In five days, the division drove inland and cleared a beachhead for supplies and troops. Driving eastward across France against fanatical resistance, the soldiers of the 1st Infantry Division spent nearly six months in continuous action with the enemy.

After capturing Aachen, the 1st Infantry Division still faced months of bitter fighting at places like the Hürtgen Forest and the Battle of the Bulge. When the War ended, the Big Red One had rolled through Germany and into Czechoslovakia.

The 1st Infantry Division remained in Germany until 1955, first as occupation troops, then as partners with the new Germany in NATO, the North Atlantic Treaty Organization. In 1955, the Big Red One redeployed to Fort Riley Kansas.

In the summer of 1965, the Big Red One was the first division called to fight in Vietnam. For nearly five years, its soldiers battled the enemy while carrying out programs to aid the people of South Vietnam.

The 4th Cavalry Squadron, to which I was assigned, is one of the most famous and most decorated squadron in the United States Army. Since its activation in 1855, the 4th Cavalry has continuously served the United States of America in peace and war. The division has fought gallantly in the Indian Wars, the Civil War, the Philippine Insurrection, World War II, Vietnam and now the Gulf War.

It was initially thought, that the terrain of Vietnam would preclude the use of armored cavalry in Vietnam. But early successes in mounted operations in the Vietnamese highlands by Troop C, 4th Cavalry, as well as successes in the area north west of Saigon known as the III Corps Tactical Zone by the 1st Infantry Division and then the 3rd Squadron, 4th Cavalry, 25th Infantry Division, convinced commanders that given their mobility and firepower, armored cavalry along with tank and mechanized infantry units supported by air cavalry could be very effective against Viet Cong and North Vietnamese forces.

The 4th Cavalry was assigned to the 1st Infantry Division as the division reconnaissance squadron based at Di An. It was the first element of the 4th Cavalry to arrive in Vietnam. The squadron's main mission was to conduct route and convoy security missions primarily along Vietnam's Route 13, the main communications and supply route from the Saigon north through Binh Doung and Binh Long Provinces. The 1st Squadron successfully accomplished this mission in the face of strong enemy resistance. It also participated in large scale combined operations such as Cedar Falls and Junction City. Overall the Quarter Horse as it was known, participated in eleven campaigns of the Vietnam War from 20 October 1965 to 5 February 1970. The 4th Cavalry was awarded a Presidential Unit Citation for its heroism in Binh Long Province as well as a Valorous Unit Award for Binh Doung Province.

In a relatively short period of time I had developed a reputation in the squadron for my professionalism, Vietnamese language skills, tactical and technical knowledge, and diligence in performing my duties. So much so that I became the *go to* guy for helping to solve difficult technical and tactical issues confronting my unit. For example, early in my tour each platoon sergeant was required to inspect and ensure that their respective 50 caliber machinegun was in perfect firing condition. When the time came to test fire the heavy and powerful weapons before the commanding officer, guns assigned to my unit was the only ones to fire without a malfunction while guns of the other units had numerous operational and mechanical problems. The commanding officer was very impressed by our results and performance and had indicated so.

Later during my tour, because of my reputation in the squadron and overall proficiency, I was given a special assignment that had never before been done in Vietnam. My assignment was to coordinate with the air force the airlift and airdrop of seven armored track units (M113 APCs), each weighing 225 tons, into a small landing zone to support an infantry unit in contact with the enemy. Two air force C130 Hercules aircrafts would be used to transport the track vehicles to a site near the Cambodian border. In total, three flights were made airlifting and transporting two vehicles each. On the first flight as the C130s approached the landing site, we came under heavy enemy ground fire and had to abort the landing. The pilot of the aircraft was reluctant to land the aircraft and wanted to cancel the flight. When he asked me my opinion, I stated to him that I was ordered by my superiors, both West Point graduates, to complete this mission so that our ground troops could have additional support in their fight against the enemy. I strongly urged him to try again. As a result, we landed safely on the second try, while still receiving ground fire. In time, we were able to get all of the track vehicles on the ground and began to engage the enemy. Soon, I was known throughout the squadron as "Platoon Daddy." I don't know how or who started the nick name for me but everyone, officers, NCO, and lower ranking enlisted men began referring to me by that name.

My unit had two primary missions during this period. The first was to provide convoy escort security and security for other army units such as engineer units working on various projects. The second, and our primary activity, while attached to infantry units, was to go on daily search and destroy missions against the Viet Cong and now forces of the North Vietnamese regular army (NVA) within our operating area called War Zone D and the Iron Triangle.

The Iron Triangle was a National Liberation Front (NLF) stronghold 20 miles northwest of Saigon, which had been built by the Vietminh twenty years before in the war against French colonialism. Serving as a supply depot and staging area with an immense underground complex including command headquarters, dining halls, hospital rooms, munitions factories, and living quarters, it was never cleared by the French, nor was it successfully neutralized by the United States or ARVN, Army of the Republic of Vietnam.

Located between Saigon, Tay Ninh, and Song Be cities, the Triangle comprised about 125 square miles and included portions of Bien Hoa, Binh Duong, Phuoc Long, Long Khanh, and Hau Nghia provinces. It was by and large bounded by the Saigon River, the Song (river) Thi Thinh north of Bien Hoa, and the Than Dien Forest in Binh Duong Province. The area was thickly forested, consisting of jungle and rubber plantations and containing a few small villages and hamlets, the most strategic being Ben Suc, which had been under NLF control since 1964.

It was at one of the many rubber plantations that my unit and I were involved in one of the biggest and most intense combat engagements of my tour in Vietnam. We had escorted an engineering and infantry units to a site where a landing field was being prepared near a rubber plantation. With my armored vehicles I had form a protective circle or perimeter around the units that resembled the way cavalry units and pioneers would circled their wagons at night in the early west for protection against the Indians. Unbeknownst to us a large enemy VC and NVA force had moved into the same area we were in. We later learned that the VC/NVA unit had attacked us by mistake because they had been given wrong coordinates for their attack. Their mission was to attack another nearby American army unit.

The fight began around 12:30 am. While standing in the turret of my tank I saw brief flashes or points of lights out in the distant night, several hundred yards away, that looked like fire flies. Next came the sounds of small arms and machine gun fire hitting the vehicles and whizzing around my head, along with the sounds of rockets and mortars hitting the ground and exploding. As the fight progressed so did the volume of noise and the amount of deadly munitions flying through the air. I was in radio communications with other members of my platoon to get a status on their situation. I stayed with my tank firing the 50 caliber and 30 caliber machineguns to return fire directly at the lights in the distance as well as directing fire for the big guns of the M48A1 tank I was on. The noise was deafening and the gray smoke from the exploding rounds of the deadly munitions gave the night air a surreal quality and sense of disbelief that anyone would be left alive after such a violent fight.

The enemy was positioned several hundred away from our position. It appears there was no attempt on their part to attempt a ground assault and try to over run our position. This was probably because they must have realized that they had attacked the wrong target and didn't know what to do once the fight had started. The fight remained very intense throughout the night and gradually waned as daybreak approached. With the first light battle damage was evident everywhere I looked. There were causalities on our side including the death of the new lieutenant that had been assigned as my platoon leader. The rest of the men in my platoon were okay.

For most of the morning and early parts of the afternoon we remained on alert in a defensive position preparing for another attack which never came. It was concluded that the enemy had withdrawn but had left their dead as the air began to be filled with the putrefied smell of corpses rotting in the hot Southeast Asian sun. Later in the day patrols were sent out from our position to survey the area. The patrols found large quantities of dead and wounded Viet Cong and

NVA soldiers in the area that had surrounded our position. The "body count" was high which indicated that they were no match for our superior firepower. The feel of victory and surviving the fight was euphoric. I was glad to be alive. For the remainder of my second tour I engaged in other similar and smaller battles and firefights against the enemy in the War Zone D area.

Another day while on a different patrol in a different part of War Zone D off of Highway 13, my armored unit came under fire from small arms and rockets off into the distance of 200 – 300 yards. The date was 23 November 1967. I was on patrol with my cavalry troop providing security for an infantry night defensive position just north of Chon Tanh. That night our camp suddenly received an intense mortar and rocket attack, followed by a massive Viet Cong ground attack. During the attack my tank was hit by a rocket round which seriously wounded two crew men and started a fire in the tank. I immediately help to move two men who were wounded outside the tank while under intense enemy small arms fire and mortar rounds exploding around me. Although I knew the fire in my tank could cause the munitions in the tank to explode, I climbed back into the tank and hurriedly put out the fire. After the fire was put out, I manned the machinegun on the tank, and while exposed to gun fire, I began to return heavy machinegun fire at the advancing enemy. After a few minutes, another rocket hit the tank starting another fire and wounding me in the eye. I then left the burning tank and ran to another tank while under heavy fire and got a fire extinguisher to, once gain, put out the fire in the tank. After putting out the fire, I manned the main gun of the tank, fully exposed to gun fire, and began returning fire toward the enemy. My actions during the battle stopped the enemy ground assault, destroyed three enemy rocket positions, and one enemy machinegun emplacement. My action also provided the impetus for our troops to mount an assault, thereby routing a much larger enemy force.

My driver, Specialist (SPC) Bey, a kid from Utah, was with me during this engagement. He helped me put out the fire, man the guns and returned fire against the enemy. When the fight was over the squadron commander Col. Seigle came to our area when he heard what Bey and I had done. He not only congratulated me but gave me an instant promotion to Platoon Sergeant or Sergeant First Class (E7). Additionally, at an awards ceremony Bey and I received the

Silver Star[20], the country's third highest award for valor in combat[21] for the actions described. The medals were pinned on our chest by commander of all U.S. and allied forces in Vietnam, General William C Westmoreland. Bey and I were probably the only two men in the entire army to have received Silver Stars for the same action while assigned to the same tank.

Bey and I had a special relationship that men have in combat. Once during the heated and intense exchange against an enemy force in which our M48A1 tank had rolled over a landmine and exploded, during the chaotic aftermath, Bey said something to me that exemplifies the camaraderie and special relationship soldiers have who experienced combat together. Bey said, "Platoon Daddy, if necessary I will give my life to try to save yours…" I said nothing in reply because I didn't know how to respond to such bravery and emotions. Why he felt a need to express this sentiment, I don't know, but as a soldier I understood his sentiments. I never forgot him and that moment.

---

[20] The Silver Star is the third-highest military decoration that can be awarded to a member of any branch of the United States armed forces for valor in the face of the enemy.
[21] See Order and Citation on page 226.

I was always compulsive about the need to be alert on guard duty because the consequences of not doing so could result in not only your death and injury to also to many others. So, it was a shock one night to see one of my men sleeping on his tank while on guard duty. To teach him a lesson I took a large bamboo stick, walked up to him while he was asleep and slammed the stick as hard as I could next to his head and against the tank. The noise must have sounded like a rifle shot as he was startled and frightfully shaken by the noise. Of course he was angry about the incident and I was angry about him being asleep. We both got into a heated argument about the infraction. The next day I was told to report to the troop commander about the incident in which I gave him my story and rationale for doing what I had done. The CO[22] agreed but advised against undertaking any similar punitive measures in the future, and the matter was dropped.

As my second tour was winding down I received order for my next assignment which was, once again, Fort Polk, Louisiana. In total disbelief that I had once again been assigned to the least favorite of any base in the entire U. S. Army, I made a request to extend my current tour in Vietnam

---

[22] Commanding Officer

for another six months instead of going to Fort Polk. The request was granted and I subsequently received a 30 days leave, which I used to visit my family and friends in the United States.

During my leave I noticed for the first time the extent to which the American society had change. Hair was longer, illegal drugs was available and used out in the open, black militancy was at its highest pitch, Muhammad Ali had refused to be drafter, and the anti-Vietnam War protect was at its zenith. Early in my career I wore my uniform because it was a symbol of pride and status, and I also wore it as form of protection against random street violence from whites. But, during my leave, for the first time, I become very self conscience of being in uniform in public because I thought whites saw me as a war monger and baby killer and blacks saw me as a traitor to my race and as an Uncle Tom fighting the white man's war. The atmosphere in 1968 in the United States was inhospitable for men and women in uniform and in a funny sense I was anxious to get back to Vietnam where I was more appreciated and felt safer.

After my return to Vietnam I was told to report to the CO. Most soldiers become nervous when they are told to report to the company commander because usually it isn't good news. I wonder if I had messed up in some way, or they found out about something I shouldn't have done, or was something wrong at home. Where my family members okay? When I reported to the CO I was told that he was going to relieve a lieutenant who was the platoon leader of another platoon and he wanted me to become the acting platoon leader until a replacement could be found. I thanked him for his confidence in me and told him that I will do my best and not let him down.

After the meeting with the CO I went back to old platoon and told them the news. They congratulated me and wished me well. I proceed to my new platoon and saw the man I was to replace. To be relieved of command is a serious black mark on a person's military records and generally has a negative impact on his or her army career. The lieutenant appeared to be crying and said he was appalled that his new replacement was going to be an enlisted man. What was evident but not said by him was that his replacement was also an African American.

To improve the comfort of my seating while on my M113 APC I had welded the metal frame of a small chair directly behind the hatch that lead down into the vehicle from the deck. With the newly welded chair frame in place, instead of standing through the port hole or hatch with one half of my body out in the open and the rest down in the vehicle, I could now sit and lean back into the chair completely outside and on top of the vehicle with my legs hanging over or across the hatch of the track. The decision to install and use the chair as I had intended was fateful as it probably saved my life.

After having the chair welded and while on patrol my platoon came under fire in broad daylight as we moved down a dirt road in the countryside. My vehicle had apparently rolled over another anti-tank mine buried in the ground which exploded under the vehicle. The massive explosion tore a large five feet by seven feet gaping hole under the vehicle instantly killing two of my men, a drive and loader, who were inside the vehicle. The force of the explosion tore off pieces of metal from the APC and combined with its own shrapnel engulf the entire of the APC and continued out through the opening on top of the track where my legs were stretched out across while sitting in the makeshift chair. The hot gases, flames, and the explosive force of the mine combined with shrapnel from the bomb and metal pieces torn from the vehicle blasted up and through the open hatch and through my outstretched legs. In turn, as the vehicle was lifted by the blast of the explosion I was simultaneously lifted up into the air and thrown off to the side of vehicle. Lying on the ground stunned and deaf from the explosion, I was unaware my legs were damaged and immediately attempted to access what had happened, the condition of my men, and the next course of action to. Lifting myself off the ground I heard many small arms fire as I attempted to climb back unto another tank. As I got on the vehicle I felt a hot sting on my right leg just above the knee and realized I had been shot. The bullet entered from the back of the leg and exited from the front. While feeling a great deal of pain caused by the bullet and the sudden realization that my legs were seriously burned and mangled, as I could now hear and feel blood gushing from my boots, I was able to reach my CO on the radio and asked for replacements to help repel the enemy, and help for the wounded and the dead. Relieved that I was able to contact my CO and give that message, I then fell to the ground and immediately loss consciousness.

What was interesting about that day is that I had convinced the platoon leader that morning into taking the day off for this patrol. Otherwise, had he not, he would have been in the lead vehicle instead of me and his track vehicle would have hit the mine buried in the ground, not my vehicle.

Had he accompanied us on the patrol he would have surely died, along with all his men, because he would have been either inside his vehicle or standing upright through the hatch with most of his body inside and exposed to receiving the full force of the mine explosion. Such is combat, a matter of chance or luck for him, or in this case the lack of either for me.

I regained consciousness just as I was being wheeled into the 24th Field Evacuation Hospital at Long Binh. As I was being wheeled in two nurses stood on either side of me with scissors in their hands. At first I was concerned because I thought they were going to use them to amputate my legs right there and then. But, smiling they said they will be used to cut off my clothes. I then became even more concerned because as a result of taking off my clothes my naked body and private parts would be exposed to the women.

I stayed at the 24th for four days. I was then airlifted to the 106th General Hospital in Yokohama, Japan for further treatment. The doctors were not optimistic about the condition of my legs during our first meeting. The damage cause by the metal fragments and fire entering from the back of both legs had caused extensive damage to the muscle and bones. The doctors insinuated that I may lose one of the legs as a result. I became concerned and depressed about my prognosis and wonder what I would do if I lost one or both of my legs. I thought about my mother and father, wife and kids, siblings, and I also thought about the choice I had made to extend my tour in Vietnam to avoid going to Fort Polk, and I thought about the wisdom of deciding to make the army a career. I prayed and decided to control my fears and wait to see what the doctors had to say on his next visit.

The next day my doctors came and told me they had good and bad news. The good news was that I would not lose my legs, that is, the legs would not been amputated. The bad news was that I would have to have extensive surgery on them, but in time I would be healthy and have full use of both my legs.

To do the surgery I had to have a spinal tap which would serve to numb my legs from the pain of the operation. At the beginning of the procedure I was visited by a psychiatrist who said he wanted to ask me just a few questions to see how I was doing. Distracted and probably just not paying attention, when the psychiatrist asked me how tall I was, I answered "9 feet 5 inches, sir". With my answer he and the other doctors knew the medication being injected into my spinal column was taking effect. The psychiatrist said "thank you" walked away, I never saw the psychiatrist again. I remained at the 106th for 17 days and was then airlifted to Walter Reed Army Hospital in Washington and home.

My war with Vietnam was over. In 1969, Richard Nixon became the new President and he had his own plan to end U.S. involvement in Vietnam. President Nixon outlined a plan called Vietnamization, which was a process to remove U.S. troops from Vietnam while handing back the fighting to the South Vietnamese. The withdrawal of U.S. troops began in July 1969. To bring a faster end to hostilities, President Nixon also expanded the war into other countries, such as Laos and Cambodia -- a move that created thousands of protests, especially on college campuses, back in America. To work toward peace, new peace talks began in Paris on January 25, 1969.

When the U.S. had withdrawn most of its troops from Vietnam, the North Vietnamese staged another massive assault, called the Easter Offensive (also called the Spring Offensive), on March 30, 1972. North Vietnamese troops crossed over the demilitarized zone (DMZ) at the 17th parallel and invaded South Vietnam. The remaining U.S. forces and the South Vietnamese army fought back.

On January 27, 1973, the peace talks in Paris finally succeeded in producing a cease-fire agreement. The last U.S. troops left Vietnam on March 29, 1973, knowing they were leaving a weak South Vietnam who would not be able to withstand another major communist North Vietnam attack.

After the U.S. had withdrawn all its troops, the fighting continued in Vietnam. In early 1975, North Vietnam made another big push south which toppled the South Vietnamese government. South Vietnam officially surrendered to communist North Vietnam on April 30, 1975. On July 2, 1976, Vietnam was reunited as a communist country, the Socialist Republic of Vietnam.

It was the longest war in American history and the most unpopular American war of the twentieth century. It resulted in nearly 60,000 American deaths and an estimated 2 million Vietnamese deaths. Even today, many Americans still ask whether the American effort in Vietnam was a sin, a blunder, a necessary war, or a noble cause, or an idealistic, if failed, effort to protect the South Vietnamese from totalitarian government.

From my point of view the Viet Cong and the North Vietnamese were remarkably different fighters than the North Koreans and the Chinese. Unlike the Koreans and the Chinese, the Vietnamese had never been conquered by any foreign powers, which freed them from the psychological constraints of being and acting like defeated people. The Vietnamese were vicious and savage fighters, much more so than we were, which is why they won the war in the end.

For my services in Vietnam I was awarded Silver Star, (2) Bronze Stars[23], (3) Purple Hearts[24], Army Commendation Medal, Vietnamese Service Ribbon, Vietnamese Campaign Medal.

---

[23] The Bronze Star Medal (or BSM) is a United States Armed Forces individual military decoration that may be awarded for bravery, acts of merit, or meritorious service. When awarded for bravery, it is the fourth-highest combat award of the U.S. Armed Forces and the ninth highest military award (including both combat and non-combat awards) in the order of precedence of U.S. military decorations.

[24] United States military decoration awarded in the name of the President to those who have been wounded or killed while serving on or after April 5, 1917 with the U.S. military.

CHAPTER 8

POST-NAM & POST-PARTUM

I arrived at Walter Reed Army Hospital in Washington, DC in July, 1968. Walter Reed is the United States Army's flagship medical center. Located in Washington, D.C., it serves more than 150,000 active and retired personnel from all branches of the military. The center is named after Major Walter Reed, an army physician who led the team which confirmed that yellow fever is transmitted by mosquitoes rather than direct contact. Since its origins, what is now the medical care facility has grown from a bed capacity of 80 patients to approximately 5,500 rooms covering more than 28 acres of floor space.

While in Japan, I underwent several surgeries to repair my legs. Because I had lost so much blood I had a number of blood transfusions which I didn't like because it made me feel uncomfortable during the transfusion process. The reason for the discomfort was because the blood I was receiving was at a lower temperature than my body temperature of 98.6 degrees. Consequently, as the blood was being infused I felt a chill throughout my body because of the cooler temperature of the blood. However, at Walter Reed, within a matter of weeks my wounds were rapidly healing and I began a daily physical therapy regime which made the process of my recovery even faster.

I shared a hospital room with a somewhat bombastic army colonel who was also injured in Vietnam. As expected we had frequent conversations on a broad range of subjects including the pros and cons of being a vegetarian, which he was an avid disciple. According to him what was currently wrong with the entire world was its reliance on meat as a source of food. He attributed most of the world's health problems including obesity, heart disease, diabetes and other blood diseases, gastro problems, sexual dysfunctions, emotional and psychological problems, and other health issues to the consumption of meat by man. He indicated he was a lifelong vegetarian and offered his own good health as proof for the validity of his claims. The colonel's argument about the benefits and virtues of being a vegetarian was rationale and intuitively made a lot of sense to me. I was so impressed by his argument and advocacy that the last time I ate meat of any kind was on 16 July 1968 at Walter Reed and I have never felt better in my life.

One day while at Walter Reed I received a telephone call from a soldier I served with in Vietnam. The caller was Colonel Seigle, my former squadron commander with the 4th Cavalry. I was glad to hear from him and appreciated the fact he was concerned about my recovery. He informed me that when I had fully recovered and left Walter Reed he had arranged for me to be reassigned to an administrative position at the U. S. Army Garrison Company located at nearly and historic Fort Myers, Virginia. I was please to hear the news because I had come to like the Washington, DC area and thought it would be a great place for me to live when I eventually retired.

Additionally, located next to historic Arlington National Cemetery, Ft Myers is not your usual army post. A very small installation, it is the home of the army's honor guard and band, and serves as the principal place of residence for all of the military's top uniform leaders including the service chiefs[25] and the joint chief[26]. Most would consider

---

[25] Service chiefs are the highest ranking officer for each of the branches and are always a four star general of admiral. They are members of the

179

assignment to Fort Myers a good duty location as I did. On my discharge from Walter Reed I received a 30-days leave which I used to resettle my immediate family into the Washington, DC area and visited with my mother and father in South Carolina.

Each army base or installation has an organization often referred to as Garrison Company. The primary mission for the unit is to be the administrative and managerial arm responsible for the operation of the physical property of the base and Issues related to maintenance, security, utilities, housing, grounds keeping, schools, churches, shopping facilities, transportation, and civilian personnel, and other base-related issues often come under the jurisdiction of the garrison company. I was assigned the noncommissioned officer in charge (NCOIC) of the 4-person training section responsible for coordinating all training activities for personnel assigned to the garrison company and certain tenant units at Fort Myers.

---

joint chiefs of staff who advises the secretary of defense on military matters.
[26] The joint chief is the chairman of the joint chief of staff and advises the president and secretary of defense on all military and national security matters.

As a combat infantry soldier this new assignment which was primarily administrative in nature was a new experience for me. I was use to being around large numbers of people handling lethal weapons of all sorts in combat zones, and in harsh terrains and climates. Now, I come to work to essentially a 8:00 am to 4:30 pm job behind a desk shuffling papers, It was all very surreal. I soon realize that I had become what I and all other combat soldiers resented and absolutely despised. I had become one of those soldiers who are assigned far in the rear of the frontlines, away from the fighting and danger, living in comfort and security with three warm meals a day, clean sheets, TVs and movies, dayrooms, and an over abundant supply of bow legged gapped teeth WACs, while combat soldiers live and fought in dirt and squalor, surrounded by constant danger. I had become an administrative supervisor. Oh, how I wished my men and friends in Vietnam who are grunts[27] could see me now.

One day after approximately four months on the job at Garrison Company I received a call to meet with the Commanding Officer and Sergeant Major of Fort Myers at

---

[27] A grunt is a common term to describe a soldier who is a combat infantryman.

Post Headquarters, along with my 1st Sergeant. I assumed it was a routine request for a meeting to discuss training or maintenance issue or some related matter. During the meeting I was told that a 1st Sergeant position was being created to replace the sergeant major at the U. S. Army Headquarters Company and because of my outstanding performance in my current assignment and my (military) record they wanted me to fill that slot. I couldn't believe what I was being told. In an instant I thought about the goal I had set for myself to someday become a 1st Sergeant years earlier I thought of all the mentors who encouraged me, and now I was about to join their ranks. I told them I appreciated their confidence and support and would do my best in the position. Despite my show of self-confidence I believe the chances of getting the appointment was slim due to my relative short length of service. I was certain other candidates with longer years of active service would be selected over me.

In the army all candidates for promotions to 1st Sergeant must appear first before the 1st Sergeants Board and be approved by that committee of senior ranking officers before receiving the promotion. After I had appeared before the board I knew I had done well and was optimistic about my chances. Two days after the board I was called to the military personnel division and was met there by Fort Myers' Post Commander and the Commanding Officer of Headquarters Company. They handed me a pair of 1st Sergeants stripes and told me to get them on right away. Although I had not fully recovered from my badly injured legs and was still experiencing pain in both of them, that day, I didn't have a problem with my legs I skipped happily down the sidewalk towards the tailor shop to have my stripes sewn on my jacket. I have made it!

The United States Army Headquarters Company, based at Fort Myers, Virginia is one of the most unique organizations in the army. It was established in 1955 and is the only company in the Army authorized its own distinctive Soldier Patch, Unit Crest and Guidon. The unit is also the largest and most diverse company in the Army with over 2500 NCOs and Soldiers assigned and attached to more than 200 DoD[28] and DA[29] agencies and staff elements within the national capital region and around the world. The company's mission is to provide the necessary leadership, command and control, administrative and logistical support,

---

[28] Department of Defense.
[29] Department of the Army.

UCMJ[30] chain-of-command authority, and training for its Soldiers.

Because of army regulations, the mission and purpose of the unit, its close proximity to senior army leadership, and the high expectations of the company's leadership group, soldiers assigned to Headquarters Company are the army's *cream of the crop*. Most soldiers assigned to the unit were handpicked either because of their extraordinary performance in the army or for a unique or specialize talent or skill their possessed before or after they had entered the army. For example, the tennis great of the 60s and 70s Stan Smith who was drafted into the army was assigned to Headquarters Company. His "job" or assignment in the army was to give tennis lessons to mostly officers' wives at the Fort Myers Officers Club. Additionally, we rarely lost a basketball, touch football, or softball game because the unit had the ability to identify noted or professional athletics entering the army and have them reassigned to Headquarters Company after they had completed their basic and advanced training.

---

[30] Uniform Code of Military Justice: the military's law statures

Another key factor which contributed to the high quality of personnel assigned was the sensitive nature and function of most the duty assignment its men and women were given. Their positions in various high-level government and military units and offices such as the army chief of staff office, office of the joint chief of staff and other service chiefs, the offices of various service secretaries, office of the Sergeant Major of the Army, intelligence and security units, and other sensitive units required individuals to have security clearances. Consequently, by definition these soldiers were better educated, more self-disciplined, less likely to have drug abuse or related problems, paid their bills, didn't beat their wives or children, and were generally all around good soldiers and citizens.

Unknown to me be before receiving my promotion and appointment a white NCO who was assigned to the office I now led was also an applicant for the position of the unit's 1st Sergeant. After I received the promotion and appointment, he immediately took leave which precluded the chance for him to provide me with an orientation to the office nor, when he returned, did he congratulate me or extend any preverbal offer of assistance should I need it. I understood his feelings and sense of disappointment at not receiving the job. After a short period of time he had transferred from the unit.

I also tracked down and placed a call to the NCO who had been my supervisor in Germany and who had given me the assignment to conduct a one hour lecture on the proper use of a screw driver. He was stationed at Fort Knox. When he wasn't available when I called, I left a message for him to return my call. I indicated in the message that it was "1st Sergeant" Dan Harper who had served with him in Germany. I called again and left the same message when he didn't return my first call. Eventually, he never returned any of my calls. I believe however, he had gotten my overall "message."

Although my family and I lived off base in Washington, DC before my promotion to 1st Sergeant, tradition and probably regulations required the 1st Sergeant of Headquarters Company to live on base at Fort Myers. I relocated my entire family to Fort Myers and we settled in Quarters 416-B, which was located next to the quarters of the Post Sergeant Major. It was a very nice and large house and my family enjoyed our stay there.

Then as now Washington, DC was the center of the political and military universe. You never knew who you would formally meet or run into by accident. Presidents, senators, congressmen, generals, admirals, presidential cabinet secretaries, ambassadors, movie stars, athletes, civil rights leaders, business tycoons, and others were always around and easy to approach as inevitably these figures would make their way onto my turf at either Fort Myers or the Pentagon. It was at this time that I first meet the senior senator from South Carolina, Senator Strom Thurman. It was easy at first to think of Strom Thurman as a staunch racist demagogue and that if it was left up to him African Americans would still be enslaved and forever remain subservient to whites as second class citizens. One needs to only review past new clippings and newsreels starting from the 1940s to see where he stood on the issue of racial equality for African Americans or any other racial or religious minorities, including Jews.

Thurman ran for president in 1948 as the segregationist States Rights Democratic Party (Dixiecrat) candidate, receiving 2.4% of the popular vote and 39 electoral votes. Thurmond later represented South Carolina in the United States Senate from 1954 until 2003, at first as a Democrat and after 1964 as a Republican. He conducted the longest filibuster ever by a lone senator in opposition to the Civil Rights Act of 1957, at 24 hours and 18 minutes in length, nonstop. In the 1960s, he continued to fight against civil rights legislation. Starting in the 1970s, he moderated his position on race, but continued to defend his early segregationist campaigns on the basis of states' rights in the context of Southern society at the time, never fully renouncing his earlier viewpoints. He switched so he could support Goldwater's conservatism and because of their shared opposition to the 1964 Civil Rights Act. He left office as the only senator to reach the age of 100 while still in office and as the oldest-serving and longest-serving senator in U.S. history (although he was later surpassed in the latter by Robert Byrd). Thurmond holds the record for the longest serving Dean of the United States Senate in U.S. history at 14 years.

That was the public side of Thurman. In time, I got to see Thurman at least once a month and he often chided me if I skipped a monthly visit with him. I found him to be thoughtful, affectionate, very personable, and sensitive. He never expressed any racial views and always treated me with respect, kindness, and affection. I was confused by Thurman's public and private sides. How could a person so caring and sensitive in private be such a monster in public? Part of the answer revealed itself shortly after he died.

Six months after Thurmond's death in 2003, it was learned that at age 22 he had fathered a daughter, Essie Mae Washington-Williams, with his family's African American maid Carrie Butler, then 16. Although Thurmond never publicly acknowledged his daughter, he paid for her college education and passed other money to her for some time. In time, Thurmond's family finally acknowledged her as a member of the family lineage. Essie Mae Washington-Williams, thus, became eligible for the Daughters of the American Revolution and the United Daughters of the Confederacy through her Thurmond lineage.

Rumors of Thurman's liaisons with African American women were prevalent throughout Edgefield, our mutual hometown. In addition to giving birth to Essie Mae Washington, he is reported to have fathered four other children in the Edgefield/Aiken area with African American women. I once asked an elderly white South Carolinian what he thought of Thurman now that it was revealed he had father a child with an African American woman. The old gentlemen said in a deep southern drawl, "oh, that shit happens all the time... you'd be surprised." He said he still like Thurman because of what he did for South Carolina and its people and held no grudge because of who he slept with. I guess I felt that way also.

Before Thurman left office he told me that he had initiated steps to have the army possibly upgrade the Silver Star awarded to me in Vietnam to the Congressional Medal of Honor[31]. I was surprised and moved by his decision to take this action on my behalf, which I did not expect nor sought. After he died, Thurman's request to the army was taken up by Maryland's senators Barbara Mikulski and Ben Cardin. As of the writing of this book, no determination has yet been made by the army and the review is still in progress.

One day, a request came down from the Office of the Army Chief of Staff to identify someone, preferably a soldier with the rank of Sergeant Major and with combat experience to serve on a three person panel that will discuss issues related to African Americans serving in the military to be

---

[31] The Medal of Honor is the highest military decoration awarded by the United States government. It is bestowed by the President in the name of Congress on members of the United States Armed Forces who distinguish themselves through "conspicuous gallantry and intrepidity at the risk of his or her life above and beyond the call of duty while engaged in an action against an enemy of the United States.

aired bi-monthly on a radio show. For reasons I will never know, although I was a 1st Sergeant, which is one rank or grade down from a Sergeant Major, I was selected to be on the panel. The two other panel members were (then) two star Major General "Chappie" James of the Air Force and one star Brigadier General Roscoe Cartwright of the Army. Both men were African Americans. General James eventually became the first African American four star general in the nation's military and General Cartwright and his wife were both killed in an airplane crash at Dulles Airport in Washington, DC in 1973. How did I as an enlisted personnel get to serve on the same panel with these high ranking officers was a conundrum to me. But I was happy to serve on the panel and gave my point of view to the best of my abilities, and with gusto and integrity.

I served as the 1st Sergeant of Headquarters Company for nearly four years. As my assignment was about to end I was told that for my next assignment I was going to be the sergeant major of an infantry battalion in South Korea. I received the news with mixed emotions. On one hand I was pleased because it meant another promotion: from 1st Sergeant to sergeant major, the highest enlisted rank. On the other hand it meant relocating to another country half way around the world without my family as South Korea was designated, then, an unaccompanied tour, meaning soldiers stationed in Korea could not bring along their families. That is no longer the case. At the same time I was hit hard by the news that my father's health was rapidly failing as he was in his 80s. While I looked forward to the promotion to sergeant major I felt a need to be near my parents in what would be their last few months or years left on this earth.

I submitted a request to the army for compassionate reassignment to an area near where my parents were in South Carolina. To my surprise my request was denied without explanation. Angry and confused I sought help from Senator Thurman to intercede on my behalf. A few hours after I met with him I was told that my request had been approved and that I would be reassigned to Fort Jackson, South Carolina when my tour was over at Fort Myers. For the first time in my army career I circumvented normal army channels to resolve an issue. Initially, I regretted taking such actions because of how it may be perceived by the army, but in the end I felt completely justified because of the seriousness of the health problems my father had and the realization that he would not have long to live. While transferring from Fort Myers to my new post at Fort Jackson, I received word that my beloved father died, on August 26, 1972, at the age of 88.

There comes a time when change eventually comes to every man or women. The change may occur gradually and very quickly. It may be physical, psychological, or spiritual, or all three. It may be caused by some unforeseen or obvious event or by circumstance such as death, divorce, and/or birth; or it may be caused by time, age, or simply the fact that you have become tired, or have lost faith, or you may begin to ask yourself questions that you have never considered or asked before. You begin to see and think differently about life, and especially your life. You also begin to feel, and feel differently about things you were always sure of. This change or turning point seems to sometime happen when a person finally reaches the goal they have for so long sought, when they finally realize it, one often asks, "what's next?"

By 1972 when I reported for duty at Fort Jackson much had changed in the world, the country, and the army. The war in Vietnam was winding down and the withdrawal of U S troops was near completion. The South Vietnamese people and army were left to their devices and had to fend for themselves. President Nixon was about to be impeached because of Watergate, the Arabs had imposed an oil embargo causing gas lines to stretch for blocks or miles, and the army was experiencing the worst morale problem ever, partly due to its perceived loss of the Vietnam War. I had also changed. The spring in my step was now gone, and not just because of my injured legs. I now began to spend a lot of time thinking about the past instead of the future, and my parents and family became my primary priority, instead of the army.

There was a perfect storm of sorts when I reported for duty at Fort Jackson. First, my positive and optimistic outlook on life began to fade as I was becoming more preoccupied and depressed over my father's death and new concerns arose about my mother's health. I visited my mother regularly and with each visit I could see she was also fading and would probably not have very long to live. I felt helpless because there was nothing I could do.

Compounding my depression over my father's death and my mother's health was that I was still disappointed and angry that despite my service and record, the army saw fit to reject my request for compassionate reassignment and was forced to seek help from Senator Thurman. I felt in light of what I had given to the army, it could have made this one concession. Adding to the hurt and disappointment caused by the army there was still more to come. One day I was called into the office of Fort Jackson's Command Sergeant Major (CSM), the highest ranking noncommissioned officer on base who reports directly to the Commanding General of Fort Jackson. When I arrived he questioned me about whether I was authorized to wear the military badges and decorations I had on my uniform. The inquiry came as a result of other NCOs on base who question how a NCO with an administrative MOS could be awarded badges and medals for valor in combat. I told the sergeant major that I was upset about the inference of his accusation and that he could have easily requested and reviewed my personnel record to verify if the decorations were authorized. I also indicated that the wearing of unauthorized badges and decorations was an offense punishable by general court martial and that I would never put myself in such jeopardy. He acknowledged everything I said and the meeting ended without an apology from him and nothing more was ever said. I assume he did check my records and discovered all was in order. The meeting with the sergeant major was a low point. It was more painful than being shot or nearly having both legs blown off.

At Fort Jackson I was the 1st Sergeant of an all female company and had responsibility for providing oversight for the first ever coed barracks in the entire United States Army. To the best of my knowledge I was the first male 1st Sergeant of an all female company. Of the total of 220 soldiers, approximately 87 were women. My CO was also a woman and career officer, Captain Patricia Harrington. In many respects this was one of my most challenging assignments ever because despite the fact that this was still the army, most or all of your preconceptions about who and what a soldiers is had to be revised and reformulated because now you are responsible for women instead of men. For example, your expectations for what a woman could do physically compared to men had to be rethought; your language and the types and degrees of profanity used had to be modified; you begin to dressed more modestly in and around the barracks; you post security in barracks between floors to keep the sexes separated; women had to be disciplined and spoken to differently than men; you had to be concerned and sensitive to the feelings of women to avoid crying and tears; and lastly you were more likely to see women engage in inappropriate behavior, of all sorts, than the men in the barracks.

One of my proudest achievements in the army was my professional behavior and conduct while being assigned to an all women's unit. Although given various offers and opportunities to fraternize with woman soldiers under my charge, I never once violated my position and office by engaging in inappropriate conduct or having unlawful relations with female soldiers in my unit.

In just a few years I had gone from being a gallant platoon sergeant of a tank unit fighting a hot war in Vietnam and a 1st Sergeant of the most important and premier company in the entire army to being questioned about the validity of the awards and badges I was authorized to wear and disciplining women soldiers caught in inappropriate behavior in the barracks on a regular basis. Something had changed and some of the fire and love for the army I had always had inside me was fading. This period was the low point of my military career.

Meaningful change like momentous decisions happens gradually. I think that is how my decision to leave and retire from the army happened. After surveying, in my mind's eye, my life, the army, and my feelings about the state of these things, my decision to leave the career I loved so much was an easy one to make. I also knew I had lost the hunger and the will to willingly endure danger, fear, physical and mental hardships, uncertainty, and the long absences from family and friends. I had come to realize that I just wanted to live an ordinary life like everyone else. Consequently, I began to think about the possibility of retiring from the army.

It was my moment of melancholy. It was my *post-partum* from Korean, Vietnam, and the army life.

We did not know about post traumatic stress syndrome (PSTD) in the early 1970s. We did not know that posttraumatic stress disorder is an anxiety disorder that can develop after exposure to any event that result in psychological trauma. This event may involve the threat of death to oneself or to someone else. As an effect of psychological trauma, PTSD is less frequent and more enduring than the more commonly seen acute stress response. Symptoms for PTSD include re-experiencing the original trauma(s) through flashbacks or nightmares, avoidance of stimuli associated with the trauma, and increased arousal – such as difficulty falling or staying asleep, anger, and hypervigilance.

In addition to the psychological disorders listed above, a substantial number of Vietnam veterans reported readjustment problems such as occupational instability, marital conflicts, and family problems. Moreover, veterans with PTSD were more likely to report marital, parental, and other family adjustment problems (including violence). Veterans who experienced the highest level of war exposure also reported the highest frequency of physical health problems.

Among Vietnam veterans, approximately 15% of men and 9% of women were found to currently have PTSD. Approximately 30% of men and 27% of women had PTSD at some point in their life following Vietnam. Vietnam veterans also struggle with a number of psychological disorders other than PTSD such as depression, anxiety, and alcohol problems, which are typically the most prevalent across groups. How could I not have PTSD?

Near the end of my term as sergeant first of the AIT unit at Fort Jackson, I received another set of orders reassigning me to Germany to be the Sergeant Major of the

14th Armored Cavalry. I was not excited about the promotion or the prospects of being assigned to another combat unit as I felt I had my share of combat duty and thought someone else should step-up to have those responsibilities.

Additionally, after being the 1st Sergeant of Headquarters Company, U. S. Army at Fort Myers, I felt that being sergeant major of a squadron, battalion, or brigade was not an equivalent assignment. At the same time my mother died October 17, 1975 at the age of 88. After much thought, although I accepted the promotion to Sergeant Major, I declined the offer to Germany and submitted my retirement papers. I formally retired from the United States Army on 31 May 1975.

EPILOGUE

I am proud of my 23-year army career as I have seen and done things most people could not possibly know or imagine. And, I have seen the very best of men and their worst, but in the end I am always hopeful that the world can be a better place, in part, because of what *good* soldiers do. In retrospect and to some extent my only regret now is that I could not continue to serve my country as a soldier.

As an African American from the segregated south the army gave me, along with many others of similar backgrounds, many opportunities to realize my full potential as a man and as a person. I have achieved numerous personal accomplishments as delineated in the book including rapid promotions early in my career, and promotion to 1st Sergeant of the premier and most important company in the entire army. I have received numerous recognitions from subordinates and superiors alike as well as decorations for combat, including the Silver Star, 2 Bronze Stars, 3 Purple Hearts, and 2 Combat Infantry Badges.

I grew up in the army and although I have always had loving parents, siblings, and family, the army essentially became another complete and involved family to me along with all the usual complications that are often found in family units. In the end, all that I am, have, and probably will be can be attributed to having joined the army in 1952.

A lot of time has withered by since I retired from the army in 1975. Upon my retirement I was a dealer for the cookware industry and marketed china, cutlery, and related products in the Washington metro area. I then spent 25 years in the retail auto industry as a sales representative, sales manager, and finally as general manager of a large auto dealership also in the Washington area.

I remarried in 2000 to a wonderful and beautiful woman the former Esther Stroy, who is not only my wife but also a partner in all my varied activities. Originally from Washington, DC, at 15 Esther became one of the youngest member of the U. S. Olympic Teams in 1968 and 1972. Esther's event was the 400 meter. She later graduated from Howard University and eventually owned and operated her own real estate appraisal agency in the DC area. We first met at a restaurant and were friends for a number of years before we married. I like to tell people that because she was an Olympian and could run fast and long distances, and we got married because she was able to *run me down*. In addition to my three children (Sabrina, Danny, and David) from my first marriage, I am stepfather to a son (Kasimu) from my marriage to my current wife, Esther, and I am also a grandfather to eight grandchildren.

Although I currently reside in the Washington metro area, I frequently travel to South Carolina to see family and friends, check on properties, and to fish, which brings me great pleasure and relaxation.

Of my 10 brothers and sisters, four brothers (James, Arthur, Leroy, Jerome, and Benny) have died. The only living brother, Clarence is a retired carpenter. Of my sisters, three (Julie Mae, Lucille, and Willie Mae) have died. Maggie Jo Jefferson is a retired educator and resides in South Carolina, and Vermelle is a retired tailor and seamstress and also resides in Philadelphia. All of my four sisters were and are the pride and joy of my heart. I have always loved and respected them and I always will.

I am a member of various veterans organizations such as the VFW, American Legion, Vietnam Veterans of Americans. However, I am not to participate as actively as I wish due to lack of time and I rather use what available time I do have with my wife and family. But, I support these groups as they are at the forefront of protecting and promoting the rights of veterans and advocating on their behalf.

There were certain known and unknown costs to making the army my career. First and foremost is the toll my decision has had on my family life. Throughout history and to this day army life has always been a challenge for spouses and children of soldiers. During Roman times, family followed their men on expeditions and to battles, encountering many hardships, even death. The most difficult challenge for military families has been the long absences and the uncertainty and fear that the absences engender, coupled by adjustment problems if and when the soldier returns. I was not immune to these issues and as a consequence, my first marriage, which produced three wonderful children, ended in divorce.

Another cost associated with my career choice has been my overall disposition toward the past and my current emotional state. For example, as with the Korean War Memorial, I have yet to visit the Vietnam War Memorial although it is just a few miles away. I believe I want to pay it a visit but even after all these years I don't think I am ready to do so yet. My thought is that I know too many men who are on that wall and I believe that the pain I would feel resulting from seeing their names, and remembering the lives lost and the surrounding tragedies it caused would be too great for me to endure at this time. It is my hope that someday I will visit the memorials for the Korean and Vietnamese wars and give honor to those who have died and suffered.

The Korean and Vietnamese wars are never far from my minds eye. The various images and peoples I knew and are associated with those wars are my first thoughts in the morning. Those images intersect and intrude into my mind and thoughts during the day whether I am working, playing, praying, arguing, relaxing, driving, loving, or in contemplation on another matter. The images are always there, around me, like the sun during the day or the dark during nights. The cold; the dead lieutenant who was the first I saw killed in combat and had to carry down the hill; the first man I killed; the hell of Pork Chop Hill; the face of the Chinese soldier who nearly bayoneted me before he was killed; the smell of rotting bodies in Vietnam; my near deaths. These and other images are my last thoughts before falling asleep and they come back and persist while I sleep in the form of dreams and nightmares. I wake up in the middle of the night, sometimes in terror other times in sorrow to be comforted by my wife Esther who somehow understands. Grunts or foot soldiers by definition kill in combat and see people die. Most often it is the case that the actions that result in death happens very close and becomes personal for these soldiers -- unlike air force pilots or navy gunners who never see the results of their actions. I contend we grunts pay a profound emotional cost that impacts negatively impacts our psyche and lives forever.

In addition to a military retiree, I am a 100-percent disabled veteran. Although still painful, my legs are usable and I am able to travel around relatively easily, albeit at times, slowly.

To the personal, emotional, and physical costs I have and am paying resulting from my wartime experiences, I can only be philosophical. The cost has been high but that is now water under the bridge. I am who I am and life is what it is. My only option at this point in my life is to endure and to continue to live the best life I can and to be a good man and person to my wife, children, other family members and friends, and to have faith that God will care for us all.

I have learned something very early in life that has helped me make it through many tough and challenging situations. That is, you can take a dollar bill and spend it anywhere you want to or anyway you want to. But, you can only spend it once. So it is in life. You can live anywhere you want to or you can live anyway you want to, but you can only live it once. Thus, it behooves us to live the best life we can and be the best that we can at all times. That is what I have tried to do.

APPENDIX A:

SUMMARY OF ACCOMPLISHMENTS

- Appointed Acting Platoon Sergeant during Basic Training at Camp Breckinridge, Kentucky.
- Promoted to Sergeant (E5) and Squad Leader less than 12 months after entering the army.
- Survivor of Pork Chop Hill
- Awarded Combat Infantry Badge, United Nations Service Medal, and Korean War Service Medal for wartime service in Korea.
- Coordinated innovative activities and personnel tracking system for unit at Fort Meade.
- Selected to serve on numerous instructor and training committees at Armor Center, Fort Knox, Kentucky.
- Selected to participate in a nine week training exercise with U. S. Army Special Forces.
- Selected to take German language course in Europe and the Vietnamese language course at Army Language School, Monterey, California.
- Selected to serve as Military Advisor to Vietnamese Ranger Battalion in Vietnam.

- Only Military Advisor to have served in three distinct capacities: Infantry Advisor, Armor Advisor, and Instructor & Trainer.
- Awarded the Bronze Star with "V" Device for Valor, (2) Vietnamese Cross for Gallantry with Palm, and Army Commendation Medal
- Handpicked by General William DePuy, commanding general of the 1st Infantry Division to join unit in Vietnam.
- Established reputation in the 4th Cavalry as the *go to guy* for solving difficult tactical problems.
- My platoon was selected to participate in first ever airdrop of armored vehicles into a hot combat zone, while under heavy ground fire.
- Survived when track vehicle was struck by landmine. Received severe wounds to face, both legs and back
- Award Silver Star for Gallantry in Action, (2) Bronze Stars, (3) Purple Hearts, Army Commendation Medal, Vietnamese Cross for Gallantry with Palm, Vietnamese Service Ribbon, Vietnamese Campaign Medal.
- Promoted to 1st Sergeant. At time of promotion, the youngest to be promoted to that rank.

- Appointed the first ever 1st Sergeant (E8) of U. S. Army Headquarters Company and the first African American and youngest to serve in that position.
- Selected by the Army Chief of Staff to serve on 3 person panel for a bi-monthly radio show that discussed issues related to African Americans serving in the military. Probably the first ever NCO to serve on a panel that included two general officers. One from the air force and one from the army.
- Selected first male 1st Sergeant of an all female company in the entire U. S. Army.
- As of this writing, nominee for the Congressional Medal of Honor.

APPENDIX B:
CHRONOLOGY OF MILITARY CAREER

Enter U S Army	September 1952
Completed BCT	December 1952
101st Airborne Division	
7th Infantry Division, Korea	January 1953
3rd Armored Cavalry, Fort Meade	March 1954
11th Armored Cavalry, Fort Knox	April 1957
3rd Armored Division, Fort Knox	March 1958
32th Regiment Instructor Committee, Fort Knox	January 1959
4th Infantry Division, Germany	January 1961
3rd Infantry Division, Germany	December 1963
5th Mechanized Infantry Division, Fort Irwin	January 1964
Military Assistance	February 1964

Command – Vietnam	
3rd Armored Division, Germany	August 1965
1st Infantry Division, Vietnam	January 1967
106th General Hospital, Yokohama, Japan	July 1968
Walter Reed Army Hospital, Washington, DC	July 1968
U. S. Army Garrison Company, Fort Myers	September 1968
U. S. Army Headquarters Company, Fort Myers	February 1969
U. S. Army Processing Center, Fort Jackson	August 1972
WAC Company, 4th Brigade, Fort Jackson, SC	February 1973
1967, Vietnam	Silver Star
1964, 1967, Vietnam	Bronze Star
1967, 1968, Vietnam	Army Commendation Medal
1967, 1968, Vietnam	Purple Heart (3)
1965	Vietnamese Cross of Gallantry with Palm (2)
1953, Korea, 1965, Vietnam	Combat Infantry Badge (2)

APPENDIX C:

RANKS OF THE UNITED STATES ARMY

Enlisted Soldiers' Ranks

PRIVATE (PVT/PV2)

(Addressed as "Private")
Lowest rank: a trainee who's starting Basic Combat Training (BCT). Primary role is to carry out orders issued to them to the best of his/her ability. (PVT does not have an insignia)

PRIVATE FIRST CLASS (PFC)

(Addressed as "Private")
PV2s are promoted to this level after one year—or earlier by request of supervisor. Individual can begin BCT at this level

with experience or prior military training. Carries out orders issued to them to the best of his/her ability.

SPECIALIST (SPC)

(Addressed as "Specialist")
Can manage other enlisted Soldiers of lower rank. Has served a minimum of two years and attended a specific training class to earn this promotion. People enlisting with a four year college degree can enter BCT as a Specialist.

CORPORAL (CPL)

(Addressed as "Corporal")
The base of the Non-Commissioned Officer (NCO) ranks, CPLs serve as team leader of the smallest Army units. Like SGTs, they are responsible for individual training, personal appearance and cleanliness of Soldiers.

SERGEANT (SGT)

(Addressed as "Sergeant")
Typically commands a squad (9 to 10 Soldiers). Considered to have the greatest impact on Soldiers because SGTs oversee them in their daily tasks. In short, SGTs set an example and the standard for Privates to look up to, and live up to.

STAFF SERGEANT (SSG)

(Addressed as "Sergeant")
Also commands a squad (9 to 10 Soldiers). Often has one or more SGTs under their leadership. Responsible for developing, maintaining and utilizing the full range of his Soldiers' potential.

SERGEANT FIRST CLASS (SFC)

(Addressed as "Sergeant")
Key assistant and advisor to the platoon leader. Generally has 15 to 18 years of Army experience and puts it to use by making quick, accurate decisions in the best interests of the Soldiers and the country.

MASTER SERGEANT (MSG)

(Addressed as "Sergeant")
Principal NCO at the battalion level, and often higher. Not charged with all the leadership responsibilities of a 1SG, but expected to dispatch leadership and other duties with the same professionalism.

FIRST SERGEANT (1SG)

(Addressed as "First Sergeant")

Principal NCO and life-blood of the company: the provider, disciplinarian and wise counselor. Instructs other SGTs, advises the Commander and helps train all enlisted Soldiers. Assists Officers at the company level (62 to 190 Soldiers).

SERGEANT MAJOR (SGM)

(Addressed as "Sergeant Major")

SGMs experience and abilities are equal to that of the CSM, but the sphere of influence regarding leadership is generally limited to those directly under his charge. Assists Officers at the battalion level (300 to 1,000 Soldiers).

COMMAND SERGEANT MAJOR (CSM)

(Addressed as " Command Sergeant Major")
Functioning without supervision, a CSM's counsel is expected to be calm, settled and accurate—with unflagging enthusiasm. Supplies recommendations to the commander and staff, and carries out policies and standards on the performance, training, appearance and conduct of enlisted personnel. Assists Officers at the brigade level (3,000 to 5,000 Soldiers).

SERGEANT MAJOR OF THE ARMY

There's only one Sergeant Major of the Army. This rank is the epitome of what it means to be a Sergeant and oversees all Non-Commissioned Officers. Serves as the senior enlisted advisor and consultant to the Chief of Staff of the Army (a four-star General).

Warrant Officers

WARRANT OFFICER 1 (WO1)

Appointed by warrant from the Secretary of the Army. WO1s are technically and tactically focused officers who perform the primary duties of technical leader, trainer, operator, manager, maintainer, sustainer, and advisor.

CHIEF WARRANT OFFICER 2 (CW2)

Chief Warrant Officers become commissioned officers as provided by the President of the United States. CW2s are intermediate level technical and tactical experts who perform increased duties and responsibilities at the detachment through battalion levels.

CHIEF WARRANT OFFICER 3 (CW3)

Advanced-level experts who perform the primary duties that of a technical and tactical leader. They provide direction, guidance, resources, assistance, and supervision necessary for subordinates to perform their duties. CW3s primarily support operations levels from team or detachment through brigade.

CHIEF WARRANT OFFICER 4 (CW4)

Senior-level experts in their chosen field. They primarily support battalion, brigade, division, corps, and echelons above corps operations. CW4s typically have special mentorship responsibilities for other WOs and provide essential advice to commanders on WO issues.

CHIEF WARRANT OFFICER 5 (CW5)

Master-level technical and tactical experts that support brigade, division, corps, echelons above corps, and major command operations. They provide leader development, mentorship, advice, and counsel to WOs and branch officers. CW5s have special WO leadership and representation responsibilities within their respective commands.

Officer Ranks

SECOND LIEUTENANT (2LT)

(Addressed as "Lieutenant")
Typically the entry-level rank for most Commissioned Officers. Leads platoon-size elements consisting of the platoon SGT and two or more squads (16 to 44 Soldiers).

FIRST LIEUTENANT (1LT)

(Addressed as "Lieutenant")
A seasoned lieutenant with 18 to 24 months service. Leads more specialized weapons platoons and indirect fire computation centers. As a senior Lieutenant, they are often selected to be the Executive Officer of a company-sized unit (110 to 140 personnel).

CAPTAIN (CPT)

(Addressed as "Captain")
Commands and controls company-sized units (62 to 190 Soldiers), together with a principal NCO assistant. Instructs skills at service schools and The United States Army combat training centers and is often a Staff Officer at the battalion level.

MAJOR (MAJ)

(Addressed as "Major")
Serves as primary Staff Officer for brigade and task force command regarding personnel, logistical and operational missions.

LIEUTENANT COLONEL (LTC)

(Addressed as "Lieutenant Colonel " or "Colonel")
Typically commands battalion-sized units (300 to 1,000 Soldiers), with a CSM as principal NCO assistant. May also be selected for brigade and task force Executive Officer.

COLONEL (COL)

(Addressed as "Colonel")
Typically commands brigade-sized units (3,000 to 5,000 Soldiers), with a CSM as principal NCO assistant. Also found as the chief of divisional-level staff agencies.

Generals

BRIGADIER GENERAL (BG)

(Addressed as "General")
Serves as Deputy Commander to the commanding general for Army divisions. Assists in overseeing the staff's planning and coordination of a mission.

MAJOR GENERAL (MG)

(Addressed as "General")
Typically commands division-sized units (10,000 to 15,000 Soldiers).

LIEUTENANT GENERAL (LTG)

(Addressed as "General")
Typically commands corps-sized units (20,000 to 45,000 Soldiers).

GENERAL (GEN)

(Addressed as "General")
The senior level of Commissioned Officer typically has over 30 years of experience and service. Commands all operations that fall within their geographical area. The Chief of Staff of the Army is a four-star General.

GENERAL OF THE ARMY (GOA)

This is only used in time of War where the Commanding Officer must be equal or of higher rank than those commanding armies from other nations. The last officers to hold this rank served during and immediately following WWII.

APPENDIX D:

ORDER FOR SILVER STAR

DEPARTMENT OF THE ARMY
HEADQUARTERS 1ST INFANTRY DIVISION
APO San Francisco 96345

GENERAL ORDERS
NUMBER 9366

28 December 1967

AWARD OF THE SILVER STAR

1. TC 320. The following AWARD is announced.

HARPER, DANIEL E ████████████████ PLATOON SERGEANT E7 United States Army

Troop C 1st Squadron 4th Cavalry

Awarded:	Silver Star
Date of action:	23 November 1967
Theater:	Republic of Vietnam
Reason:	For gallantry in action against a hostile force: On this date, Sergeant Harper was serving as a platoon sergeant with an armored cavalry troop. His unit was providing security for an infantry night defensive position north of Chon Thanh. Late at night, the camp suddenly received an intensive mortar and rocket barrage, followed by a massive Viet Cong ground attack. During the initial barrage, Sergeant Harper's tank was struck by a rocket round which seriously wounded two crew members and started a fire in the turret. He unhesitatingly helped move the two casualties outside of the tank, ignoring the intensive automatic weapons and mortar fire raking the area as he did so. Although he realized that his ammunition might explode at any moment, Sergeant Harper, with complete disregard for his personal safety, climbed back inside the tank and put out the fire. He then took an exposed position atop the turret and began placing heavy machine gun fire on the advancing insurgents. After a few minutes, another rocket hit the vehicle, wounding him and again setting fire to the turret. Disregarding his wounds, Sergeant Harper braved the hostile fire as he ran 30 meters to another vehicle to secure a fire extinguisher. After putting out the fire, he again took an exposed position atop the tank and directed the fire of his main gun against the insurgents. In addition to stopping many ground assaults, he was responsible for destroying three rocket positions and one automatic weapons emplacement. His courage under fire and his bold leadership were instrumental in enabling his unit to rout a numerically superior Viet Cong force. Platoon Sergeant Harper's unquestionable valor in close combat against numerically superior hostile forces is in keeping with the finest traditions of the military service and reflects great credit upon himself, the 1st Infantry Division, and the United States Army.
Authority:	By direction of the President, as established by an Act of Congress, 9 July 1918, and USARV Message 16695, dated 1 July 1966.

APPENDIX E:

NEWS CLIPPING OF CAPTAIN TEMPLETON

Geoffrey B. Templeton
NASA Quality-Control Official

Geoffrey B. Templeton, 68, an Army major and decorated veteran of the Vietnam War who became a quality-control official at NASA, died of an embolism June 8 at his home in Emmett, Idaho.

Maj. Templeton served 24 years in the Army and volunteered for four tours of duty in Vietnam. He received the Silver Star for leading a company of soldiers through a reconnaissance mission under enemy fire in October 1968.

He refused evacuation despite severe wounds, helped in the evacuation of other casualties and directed the efforts of his soldiers "until a successful assault was launched and victory was assured," according to the award citation.

His other decorations included the Distinguished Flying Cross, the Bronze Star Medal and the Purple Heart.

Maj. Geoffrey Templeton won the Silver Star in Vietnam.

After the war, Maj. Templeton was an officer in the Army's armored branch and settled in the Washington area. He retired from the military in the mid-1980s.

He spent 17 years at NASA and oversaw a program that monitored the quality of contractors. He retired in 2003.

He was a former member of St. Anthony of Padua's Catholic Church in Falls Church. After his NASA retirement, he moved to Idaho from Arlington County.

Geoffrey Becton Templeton was born in Los Angeles, where his family was involved in moviemaking for generations. His father was a film and television producer and director.

Mr. Templeton was a 1962 graduate of the Georgetown University School of Foreign Service and served as junior-year class president.

To order this book or for additional information,

please contact:

Daniel Harper

HARPER PRESS

6314 Brinkley Court

Temple Hills, Maryland, 20748

USA

Telephone: (301) 449-4476

Email: dharper@harperpress.com

URL: www.harperpress.com